THE WAR OF DREAMS

Anthropology, Culture and Society

Series Editors:
Dr Richard A. Wilson, University of Sussex
Professor Thomas Hylland Eriksen, University of Oslo

THE WAR OF DREAMS
EXERCISES IN ETHNO-FICTION

MARC AUGÉ

Translated by Liz Heron

Pluto Press
LONDON • STERLING, VIRGINIA

First English edition published 1999 by Pluto Press
345 Archway Road, London N6 5AA
and 22883 Quicksilver Drive,
Sterling, VA 20166–2012, USA

Published with assistance of
the French Ministry of Culture

Published in French as
La Guerre des rêves: exercices d'ethno-fiction
Copyright © Éditions du Seuil 1997
Collection *La Librarie du XXe Siècle*,
sous la direction de Maurice Olender

This translation © Liz Heron 1999

British Library Cataloguing in Publication Data
A catalogue record for this book is available from
the British Library

ISBN 0 7453 1389 2 hbk

Library of Congress Cataloging in Publication Data
Augé, Marc
　　[Guerre des rêves. English]
　　The war of dreams : exercises in ethno-fiction / Marc Augé
translated by Liz Heron.
　　　　p.　cm.
　　Includes bibliographical references.
　　ISBN 0–7453–1389–2
　　1. Anthropology—Philosophy. 2. Anthropology—Methodology.
3. Symbolic anthropology. I. Title.
GN33.A8213　1999
301'.01—dc21
99–14273
CIP

Designed and produced for Pluto Press by
Chase Production Services, Chadlington, OX7 3LN
Typeset from disk by Stanford DTP Services, Northampton
Printed in the EC by TJ International, Padstow

CONTENTS

... soñemos, alma, soñemos
otra vez; pero ha de ser
con atención y consejo
de que hemos de despertar
de este gusto al mejor tiempo ...

(... let us dream, my soul, let us dream
again; but we must be mindful
and not forget
that when the time comes
we must awaken from this delight ...)

(Pedro Calderón de la Barca, *La vida es sueño*,
Third day, scene 5)

LOOK OUT!

During the Cold War years there was an American television series called *The Body Snatchers*. Its hero, David Vincent, had witnessed extra-terrestrials landing one night and stumbled across their secret – this establishing moment was re-run at the start of every episode. The nature of the body snatchers' plan was in fact to take over our planet through an operation of total substitution: by replicating their appearance in every way, they were stepping into the shoes of the humans they eliminated, though as far as I can remember there was one tell-tale detail that sometimes enabled those in the know, David Vincent in particular, to distinguish the copies from the originals: through some freakish flaw in this extra-terrestrial technique, the little finger on the left hand of the replacement humans was peculiarly stiff. These clones from outer space moreover possessed all the requisite information about the politics and science of the earthlings (at any rate those from the United States, who, the general thrust of the series seemed to imply, represented the simultaneous quintessence and totality of human civilisation) and about the individuals whose physical appearance they assumed and whose personality traits they reproduced. This substitution strategy posed countless problems for David Vincent, for one thing because he came up against widespread scepticism among those to whom he turned to give notice of the impending danger, and because at the same time he was never completely sure that they were who they were.

1

It even sometimes happened that he would un-mask one or other of those who were seemingly his friends by suddenly realising (that little finger again!) that he was only a fake working for the takeover.

It was easy and no doubt justified at the time to see in this series the expression of certain American fantasies and a metaphorical (metaphorical at a pinch) denunciation of the Communist presence which was alleged to threaten and subvert world freedom and the stability of the United States – in the guise of scholars and artists, or apparently ordinary wholesome and patriotic citizens. But the fable was a powerful one and the solitude of its hero, made every day more acute by the blindness of some and the deception of others, had an unquestionably tragic side. Each episode, however, would have a fairly happy ending – the series had to keep going. David Vincent would miraculously extricate himself from the most hazardous situations. As for the aliens, by a stroke of luck, they would turn out to be susceptible to the effect of plain old human guns, almost instantaneously melting away into thin air whenever the bullets hit them. The Communist presence would in the end, we all knew, show itself to be made of the same feeble stuff.

Why am I harking back to this series? Because it strikes me, paradoxically, as an apt symbol for a different invasion happening all over the Earth to varying degrees, one unnoticed by many and underestimated by those aware of its existence. Its agents' faces are well-known, be they bland or prestigious. We think we know them yet, most of the time, we make do with finding them familiar ('Haven't I seen you somewhere on TV?'). This, you will have guessed by now, is the invasion of images, but in a much wider sense it is the new regime of the imaginary which nowadays touches social life, contaminating and penetrating it to the point where we mistrust it, its reality, its meaning and the categories (identity, otherness) which shape and define it.

Without making any claim to be quite so effective as the now mythic hero of the American series, I want, like him, to try and uncover the tracks of the anonymous invasion those effects we are beginning to experience without any clear perception of its causes. This book is therefore intended to be an investigation, an anthropological investigation.

This will not be exhaustive. It will be more a case of bringing together a number of instances which are often perceived in isolation and thereby giving them some starting point for meaning. We can deplore the fact that children (and quite a few adults) spend too much time in front of the television set, but we can relativise the scope of the observation by noting that this overindulgence leads to lethargy or that talking about last night's programmes with other people is also a way of creating sociability. We can display some scepticism or be appalled by the idea that romances can be formed on the Internet and that having conversations with faceless interlocutors is becoming the norm, but we can be consoled by the thought that, like the fax machine, the Internet is a salvation for writing. We can alternately and contradictorily smile or shudder at the possibilities for virtual tourism to be offered by the three-dimensional images which will soon invade computer screens, then tell ourselves that after all it's not as if things are too good to be true and a fondness for pictures has never stopped anyone from going for a stroll alongside the realities they reproduce. We can be astounded by the uniformity of the landscapes and settings which goes hand in hand with the widespread growth of big hotel chains, major motorway developments or international airports, by the artificial nature of amusement parks, *circences* for the use of the planet's new *petite bourgeoisie*, but we can simultaneously reflect that these stereotypes are the price to be paid for opening up the world to a greater number of human beings. We can ... there are a lot of things we can do all in all, for example we can also ask ourselves about the fashion for talk shows on television, we can list and decry, be it with fury, irony, scepticism or indulgence, the instances of aesthetic disaster and bad taste pandered to which litter the Earth, or the increasing insulation of the well-to-do classes who with every day that goes by close themselves off more and more in their electronically controlled buildings, their exclusive urban areas, and their private beaches – the fortresses and ivory towers of an extremely paradoxical 'globalisation'. The respective objects of these assorted observations may provoke laughter, smiles or disgust. But it is once the fine connection running between them is identified that disquiet can arise.

Bringing this connection to light is a matter for anthropology. Through the study of different institutions or representations, social anthropology has always had as its object the relationship between each one of them, or to be more precise, the different types of relationship which every culture authorises or imposes by making them thinkable and manageable, in other words by symbolising them and institutionalising them. We should add that cultures have never dropped out of the sky, that the relationships between human beings have always been the product of a history, of conflicts, of power relations. The need for them to make sense (thinkable and manageable social sense) does not make them correspond to natural necessities, even when they appear to do so.

In view of the facts as they apparently stand today, and in view of the apparent fact, contradicting them without dismantling them, of a crisis of meaning – in symbols and institutions – anthropology, one might go so far as to say by definition, is called upon to ask a few questions. And the hypothesis of the investigating anthropologist is that the different manifestations of the current crisis have something in common, that they are clearly the diverse but associated symptoms of a single phenomenon, of a single aggression.

The anthropologist has certain means at his disposal in order to carry out his investigation and, at the very least, to clarify his hypothesis. The Western ethnographic tradition has been interested in images, those produced by others: their dreams, their hallucinations, their possessed bodies. It has observed and analysed the way in which these images derived all their meaning from within shared symbolic systems, the way in which they were reproduced and sometimes modified through ritual activity. Anthropology has been interested in the individual imagination, in its perpetual negotiation with collective images; in the making also of those images or rather of those objects (sometimes called 'fetishes') which appeared both as producers of images and as social connection. Anthropologists, moreover, have had the opportunity (to be exact, they have not been able to avoid it) of observing, through situations coyly described as 'cultural contact', how confrontations of the imaginary accompanied the clash of nations, conquests and colonisations, and how resistances, withdrawals and hopes took shape in the imagination of the vanquished for all that it was lastingly affected by, and in the strict sense imprinted with, that of the victors.

On this terrain, the anthropologist has allies, historians for a start. Historians, more specifically those with what one might call a pronounced adherence to the current known as 'historical anthropology', have turned their attention on the Church's active efforts – throughout a period which Jacques Le Goff has described as a ' long Middle Ages' – to alter the dreams and re-fashion the imagination of peoples imbued with paganism who, moreover, still find today that the enduring rapture of their world gives them a wealth of meanings and makes their lives purposeful. Historians have had other areas of inquiry and anthropologists should be grateful to those who, while working in Mexico, Central America and South America, have been able to analyse in minute detail the complex effects of the lengthy attack carried out by Christian imagery against cultures which have themselves given images their due.

Other disciplines have plainly played a crucial part in the realm of the image, its production, its reception, its influence, its relation to dream, to reverie, to creativity and fiction. Psychoanalysis, Freud at any rate, and semiology, especially when it is avowedly offered as a continuation of psychoanalytic inquiry, are anthropology's natural allies in this domain.

I referred a bit earlier to a 'new regime of fiction'. In fact the image is not the only issue in this register of change which we are invited to establish today. More precisely, it is the conditions of circulation between the individual imagination (for example, the dream), the collective imagination (for example, myth) and fiction (literary or artistic, visually constituted or otherwise) which have changed. Now it is because the conditions of circulation between these different axes have changed that we can ask ourselves fresh questions about the actual status of the imagination. One question that can be asked is about the threat posed to the imagination by the systematic 'fictionalisation' to which the world is subjected, and this turning into fiction itself depends upon a set of power relations which is very concrete and very perceptible, but those terms are not easy to identify. To put it in a nutshell, we all have the feeling that we are being colonised but we don't exactly know who by; the enemy is not easily identifiable; and one can venture to suggest that this feeling now exists all over the world, even in the United States.

This idea of ours is therefore something different from that straightforward denunciation of the cyber-world which is common enough nowadays. This denunciation, indeed, has its prophets and its critics or its sceptics. On the side of the 'prophets', Paul Virilio has insisted, in various works of his, on several disturbing aspects of modern technologies which set up relations to the world predominantly in terms of instantaneity and ubiquitousness, while simultaneously prompting visions of human bodies in solitude and immobility, bodies bristling with prostheses, of de-urbanised cities and de-historicised societies. Others have pointed out on the contrary (I have in mind an article by François Archer in *Liberation*, 22 May 1996) that we have never moved around so much as we do today; that is, there is a developing sociability among the middle strata of society; that museums, historic sites and leisure parks are seeing an unprecedented success; in short that we must be on our guard against the apocalyptic forecasts of the prophets of the virtual.

This is not the place for us to enter into that debate. At any rate not through the same door. Every generalised prophecy that is based on a single sector of the social, even when it is a sector as spectacularly developed as that of the communication technologies, is plainly reckless because it necessarily underestimates the sociological plurality and complexity of innovation within a global totality which is still broadly diversified. On the other hand, any easygoing observation of the fact that 'life goes on' and that it is even more actively cultural than it was yesterday is both partial and inadequate: the social instances upon which it rests are located within the most advantaged countries or classes, and they should be analysed as such. Perhaps what has changed is more accurately how people travel, how they look at things and how they meet, thus confirming the hypothesis whereby the global relationship between human beings and the real is altering under the influence of representations connected with the development of technologies, with the globalisation of certain key issues and with the acceleration of history. At this point we shall do no more than recall one general observation as a way of bringing to mind a specific question. The general observation is that all societies have lived in and through the imagination. We can say that in every case the real would be 'hallucinated' (the object of individual or group hallucinations) if it were not symbolised, in other words collectively represented. The specific question concerns how we know what happens to our relationship with the real when the conditions of symbolisation change. That was David Vincent's question but, to his misfortune, none of his interlocutors formally acknowledged its premiss – a changed symbolic, or, if we prefer, a changed cosmology. They thought he was hallucinating (he saw aliens everywhere) whereas he was witnessing the installation of the new order. The real hallucinators were in fact his detractors, who, by confusing reality with appearance, were mistaking aliens for good Americans, the moon for green cheese. We in our turn shall try to find some symptomatic value in a paradoxical phenomenon: the impotence of symbolisation at the very moment when globalisation could give us instead the feeling that we have 'seen all there is to see' of the world and its inhabitants and that our relationships with one another are at last reaching their full meaning. If here the medical metaphor combines with the metaphor of war it is because the enemy is within us, already deep inside the fortress, intra- rather than extra-terrestrial, and that is what is perverted in our perception, our difficulty in establishing and conceiving of relationships (what we sometimes call crisis) derives more from a disturbance in our immune system than from any external aggression. Our sickness is auto-immune, our war is civil.

THE NUB OF THE SITUATION
THE PERCEPTION OF THE OTHER IN OUR TIME

The current period bears witness to the development of a quite singular paradox. On the one hand, powerful unifying or homogenising factors are at work on this Earth: economics and technology become daily more global, business conglomerates operate on a multinational scale, new forms of economic and political co-operation bring nation states closer; images and information circulate at the speed of light, certain kinds of consumerism have a market that is planet-wide. On the other hand, we can see empires and federations breaking up, local characteristics being affirmed, nations and cultures asserting their autonomous existence, religious or ethnic differences being invoked with such rupturing force that they can lead to murderous violence.

This observation can be supplemented by at least two others: the importance of migratory movements, to explain the unequal economic, demographic and political situations between different countries, and the expansion of the urban fabric, which is conspicuous on every continent. Thus the paradox observed at the global level (the paradox formed by the co-existence of homogenisation and specific characteristics) is to be found at a local level: the upper reaches of economic and technological development which take the planet in its totality as their field of action (in this regard a planet which is made uniform, treated as a market, an area for expansion, a site of competition or partnership) are usually those where different origins, languages and cultures co-exist in a quite spectacular manner.

This mixture of unity and diversity appears all the more disconcerting for being reproduced and proliferated by the mass media which are simultaneously its expression and one of its agents. There is nothing metaphorical in our customary use of the terms 'spectacle' and 'look' in relation to it. It is indeed our look which is driven wild by the spectacle of a culture dissolving in quotations, copies and plagiarism, of an identity losing itself in images and reflections, of a history which is swallowed up in the here-and-now and of a here-and-now which is itself indefinable (modern, postmodern?) because we perceive it only piecemeal, without any organising principle which can enable us to give meaning to the clichés, advertising commercials and commentaries which stand in for our reality.

What conclusion can the anthropologist derive from this in terms of his empirical objects of inquiry, and, even more so, in terms of the intellectual construction of his object? The question of otherness is central here, it has always been so for anthropology, but in our time it can be all the more starkly separated out: the anthropologist must certainly identify others (those whom he studies) and ask himself questions about their relationship to otherness, about the way in which they themselves conceive their relationship to the others who are close to them or far from them. The terms of this double undertaking have changed: neither the identification of the 'others' to be studied, nor conceptions of the other which operate in contemporary societies, are what they were at the start of the century. The question of otherness is seldom posed as such. It is rather the problematic kernel of the apparently more sociological notions and the more popularised usage we find in the notions of identity, culture and modernity. The question of identity is posed always in relation to the *other*.

Probably this is the very reason why, at the start of voyages of discovery, exploration and ethnology, the question of identifying the others to be studied or to be colonised was never asked. In the eyes of a West which, in this relation, never interrogated its own internal alterities, all of those whom it discovered, whom it colonised and whom it observed were others. The colonial powers were rivals and they clashed violently at times. But what they had in common was a recognition of the radical otherness of those over whom they clashed. From this standpoint, one could advance the idea that the colonial enterprise as a whole was an opportunity for the countries of Europe to reach an awareness of their identity: as rivals among themselves, but as different from those whom they undertook to enslave and convert. A philosopher as renowned as Leibnitz had moreover urged them to make peace among themselves and turn their weapons on other continents.[1] He was heard on only the second of these points.

At the ethnological level, it would be possible to demonstrate that all ritual activity has the goal of producing identity through the recognition of alterities. Rituals of birth, initiation rituals and funerary rituals all stage an Other (generations, an ancestor, a god or a sorcerer) with whom it is necessary to establish or re-establish an appropriate relation in order to assure the status and existence of the individual or the group. Within what might be an excessively functionalist and Durkheimian perspective certain ethnologists have gone so far as to say that the avowed purpose of the ritual was not its true purpose. But it is probably unnecessary to deny the 'performative' value of the ritual in order to recognise its 'identifying' value. Besides, when it comes to rituals, union, and even more so awareness of union, makes strength. Those who wish to cure an individual or call up a curse through the celebration of the ritual, genuinely wish for it but in order to do it they need to construct some external (other) point of reference in relation to which they identify themselves as the same (internal and identical). Moreover, a ritual specialisation is a factor of identification and recognition in the eyes of those who are not included in it.

We can therefore maintain that ritual activity creates identity and is not just its translation. I made my debut as an ethnologist on the Ivory Coast in a group of some 10,000 individuals. The Ivory Coast is well known for the large number of ethnic groups which compose it and of languages which are spoken there. These ethnic groups are often the result of inter-mixing within the population; some observers have even been able to maintain that, by imposing a single name and a single administration on composite groupings, the colonial intervention thereby hardened the contours and modified the nature of the existing population. The group I studied had a name (Alladian); within it a single language was spoken; the language of some but not all neighbouring groups was understood. The foundation histories of the villages and the settlement of subgroups did not conceal the heterogeneity of the population, even if a common point of departure had been assigned to the different migrations – in some sense this is an external and shared historical instance; there had been no common political authority recognised there before the colonial authorities created a district chief whose jurisdiction coincided roughly with that of the 'Alladian' villages, and before the national authorities created an overall chief of the Alladians, someone who had no historical precedents but was the uncle of a leading political personality.

Added to this diversity of origins there was what one might call an internal ethnic diversity. Where the Alladians live is between the sea and the lagoon some 100 kilometres from Abidjan. Ever since the sixteenth century they have monopolised trade with the Europeans. The great trading dynasties conducted the sale of numerous products from the interior (palm oil first and foremost, in the second half of the

nineteenth century) to the Europeans, and conversely, they sold
sea salt and manufactured European products to the interior.
Their wealth was translated into the purchase of numerous
slaves originating from the Centre and the North. In this
matrilineal society the acquisition in large numbers of women,
bought or dowried, guaranteed the Alladian notables an agnatic
line of descent over which they had the same rights as they did
over those descended from the mother's womb. This
movement of integration and reproduction was accentuated in
the nineteenth century, so much so that nowadays there is no
Alladian lineage that can lay claim to any kind of ethnic 'purity'.

This meant that Alladian unity was linguistic (without any
translation into politics) but it was expressed above all at the
ritual level, with one of the coastal villages of a major trading
dynasty holding a monopoly on the cult of certain marine
divinities. On the occasion of certain feasts, all the Alladian
villages and dynasties would be represented and this gathering
– whose immediate aim was to appease the powers of the sea
in order to favour fishing and trade – was clearly an opportunity
for reinforcing matrimonial alliances, for harmonising trading
policies, for exchanging news, in short for stating at regular
intervals the need for some kind of identity. Sometimes among
the participants at the feasts were those known as the 'water
people', which is to say different ethno-linguistic groups
occupying the territory of the lagoon and the coast adjacent
to the Alladians and having certain interests in common with
them, sometimes antagonistically. The ritual space therefore
went beyond the linguistic frontiers. Today, in a different
context, in an Ivory Coast which is independent and headed
by a president, there is a tendency within the lagoon area for
a certain political awareness to be displayed towards other
groups; it can moreover promote that national integration
which could otherwise be threatened by the claims of
demographic groups that are much more powerful.

One cannot overstress the importance of ritual activity in the elaboration of relative identities – in this particular case dynastic, specific village, ethnic or regional identities. We see it equally at work in the integration rituals of slaves of external origin or in the rituals shared by the Alladian subgroups and sometimes by other groups. The social bond created by the ritual must be thinkable (symbolised) and manageable (set within an institution); in this sense the ritual is a mediator, a creator of symbolic and institutional mediations which allow the social actors to identify with others and to differentiate themselves from them, in short to establish bonds of meaning (of social meaning) between them.

Two observations should be made in relation to this: whenever a ritual blockage is produced, a symbolic deficit, a weakening of mediations – of the cosmologies or 'intermediary bodies' of which Durkheim spoke – which is to say an interruption or a slowing down of the identity/alterity dialectic, signs of violence make their appearance. The second observation is this: new techniques of communication and image-making render the relation to the Other more and more abstract; we become accustomed to seeing everything but there is some doubt whether we are still looking. The substitution of media for mediations thus contains within it the possibility of violence. But the development of media and the changes which affect communication and the image are changes most usually presented as cultural and it is normal by now to ask oneself about the role of culture or the idea which one forms of it most recently in history.

The most intensely controversial events in the here-and-now are marked by the proposing of notions such as culture and religion. I shall say that it is according to the capacity of movements described as 'cultural' or 'religious' to elaborate rituals, which is to say to stimulate the identity/alterity dialectic, that we can measure their chances of influencing the future.

We know, for example, the importance of the religious movements developing today in Central and South America. Some of them make explicit reference to an ethno-cultural dimension, like the new 'Mayan religion' in Guatemala. It strikes me that the important thing in relation to movements of this kind is not to focus on the somewhat mythified or idealised aspect of the past to which they make reference, but to measure their capacity for creativity and openness in the present. The re-created past is the great historical Other in relation to which a present identity can be stated. The difficulty, one both ritual and political in nature, resides in the necessary dual negotiation, first with others who are close (those who can also likewise call themselves 'Mayans') and with others who are further away (those who lay no claim to any Indian past). The difficulty is real since we have many examples of ethno-cultural resistance movements which have not succeeded in going any further than the context of their initial statement of singularity.

Before proceeding, I should like quickly to refer to two current conflicts both regarded as 'ethnic', in order to underline the significance of the ritual or symbolic capacity which I have just spoken about. In an interview given to the newspaper *Le Monde*, the writer, Yachar Kemal, of Turkish nationality, affirmed: 'I do not think that the Kurds would wish for independence if they secured their cultural rights.'[2] Yachar Kemal is of Kurdish and Turkmen origin; in his childhood he listened to the Kurdish legends and the tales of the Turkmen troubadours. He is therefore in a paradoxical situation since he has been sentenced several times by his country's judicial system, even though he denies being a Kurdish nationalist, and is at the same time the most popular writer in Turkey. For Yachar Kemal there is an incompatibility between feudalism, which still exists among the Kurds, and nationalism; nationalism has been provoked by the excesses of the political repression of the Turkish state. In his view a Kurdish identity could be maintained in the midst of a truly democratic Turkey: 'There are countless ways of helping Turkey to become democratic, by means of debate, mediation, and political pressure.' Yachar Kemal sees political pressure coming most specifically from Europe and what he indicates for us, through his triple reference to the existence of a Kurdish identity, to an internal openness and a call for a European dimension, is clearly that the nature of the identity/alterity pairing is both necessary and relative. In terms of culture, of which his personal conception has been in both the most literary and the most popular forms, he adds: 'there has always been interaction between cultures. Lévi-Strauss helped me to understand this.' He is probably referring most specifically to *Race et Histoire*, that text in which Lévi-Strauss explains Europe's remarkable efflorescence during the Renaissance through its open reception of the most diverse and distant cultural traditions.

Let us bear in mind that Yachar Kemal's very relative optimism is tied to his hope that one can still believe in the establishment of a system of mediation in Turkey – in this instance I would be willing to refer to democratic rituality. With regard to the Chechens, the anthropologist and historian Georges Charachidze demonstrates a much more radical pessimism. In a contribution to the same issue of *Le Monde,* he draws attention to the Russian power's very long-standing refusal to negotiate with a populace which it intends to eliminate: 'As early as 1834 in imperial Russia, one bureaucrat wrote: "The only thing to be done with this ill-intentioned populace is to eliminate it down to the very last one." Boris Yeltsin recently declared: "They are mad dogs, we must cut them down like mad dogs."' For its part, Charachidze tells us, the Chechen people has its back to the wall: 'Its survival today is a matter of its existence as a Nation. Remaining inside Russia means the certainty of disappearing as a people.' Chechenya is clearly an example of the impossibility of mediation; enforced violence.[3]

What place then does a culture have in this history made up of negotiations or acts of violence? First and foremost, quite clearly, culture does not inherently imply any refusal or incompatibility, in so far as it remains culture, which is to say, something creative. A culture which goes on reproducing itself exactly (a culture of the reservation or the ghetto) is a sociological cancer, a death sentence, just as a language which is no longer spoken, which no longer borrows and no longer invents, is a dead language. There is therefore always a certain danger in wishing to defend or protect cultures and the search for their lost purity is somewhat illusory. They have only ever been alive in so far as they transformed themselves.

That said, we can raise questions about the conditions of their transformation. Living cultures are receptive to outside influences; in one sense all cultures have been contact cultures; but it is what they make of these influences that is interesting. We sometimes are inclined to regard culture and ethnicity as reflections of one another, turning the intangibility of the former into the condition of the latter's existence. Within this perspective any penetration from the outside is regarded as de-culturation and all de-culturation as de-socialisation, a loss of identity. If on the contrary we take into account that all culture is living, then contact, and the testing out of the other, are rather an opportunity for confirmation: what are the reactions of the culture in contact? Does it give signs of life or signs of weakness? The answer is often ambiguous.

I have had the opportunity to make several visits to a Pumé-Yaruro group in Venezuela, not far from the Colombian frontier. It was one of my students, Gemma Orobitg, who was staying and working among these Indians, in collaboration with Venezuelan colleagues. The Pumé are interesting in more than one respect but here I shall confine myself to two aspects of their current way of life. They live in poverty, as outcasts, ground down by *criollo* stockbreeders, in areas of the plain were the land is poor and game is scarce. With next to no aid, they live in great isolation. They have always resisted Christian preaching and even today they carry out an intense ritual and dream activity, principally on the occasion of a ceremony celebrated several nights a week, the *tohe*, which gathers them around a singing shaman, in Spanish a *cantador*. For the Pumé, one single individual can unite several distinct personalities, which are known as a *pumetho*. It is obviously the most powerful and most prestigious individuals who possess several *pumethos*. The shaman, whose body is one of the *pumetho*, one of the personalities, remains present throughout the ceremony, while simultaneously travelling with another of his *pumethos*, another of his personalities, into the world of the gods, where he reclaims sick Pumé, meets with ancestors or speaks with the gods. While he is travelling, the *tohe* goes on in the village and, around midnight, one or other of the gods comes down, approaches the *cantador* and, supposedly, sings in his place (when the voice of the shaman–singer is it at its strongest and most beautiful, it is said that the gods are singing). This quasi-possession, this vocal possession, parallels the journey, the waking dream of the shaman. But if the possession must be forgotten, the dream must be remembered, and Gemma Orobitg has collected a great many tales (some of these in my presence) of shaman journeys or dreams in the current sense of the word. Now here is the remarkable thing: the Pumé have always had a good knowledge of their mythology, they make living portraits of their gods, and their dreams are rich, but in their tales, the influence of the outside world and the images of the outside world are startling. The world of the gods is described as a hyper-modern city in which there are cars or silent, automatic aeroplanes flying around; there is an enormous abundance of consumer goods, the streets are wide and well lit, the buildings tall and shining. The world of the gods is, in short, a transfigured vision of Caracas. In the village there are two Pumé who briefly saw something of Caracas on a trip there for medical care; apart from that, a few newspaper photos, a few echoes from a transistor radio, a car or a small motor boat passing through from time to time, a plane glimpsed in the sky, have been enough to feed their dreams and their imagination. But it seems to me that this is precisely why one can describe their mythology as a living one. Of course mythologies speak of origins but these are cited, used, explored and re-imagined in order to answer the questions asked by the present. Pumé mythology's capacity to integrate everything that the Pumé can imagine of a world which paradoxically eludes them the more they feel it becoming daily less remote (when, for example, the candidate for election as governor comes round on tour) is a sign of vitality, of sensitivity to the global environment.

Mythology is only one part of culture. But it is a very resilient part. This does not alter the fact that the Pumé are in the process of disappearing as a group. Even so they clearly define their identity in social and cultural terms and seem to attach little importance to the fact that many of them are of mixed ancestry – a lot of the Pumé have been killed and many of the Pumé women raped in the course of the century. In one sense it is the *tohe* which makes the Pumé. But the Pumé have a fragile demography; some of them have left for the outskirts of the city where they have discovered a different kind of poverty. Those who remain are aware of this threat of extinction and express it in their way, in the language of mythology, with the acknowledgement that the gods are growing more distant and coming down to visit them less often. We could therefore say simultaneously that their culture is living (at least in the aspects of myth and ritual) but that their identity is disintegrating. For if they have fewer and fewer interlocutors at the cultural level, they have none at all at the social level.

Perhaps here we have a process which is to some extent the reverse of what happened in the process of Catholic pros-elytising and colonisation in Mexico. Serge Gruzinski has carefully analysed the conditions in which, from the sixteenth century on, the mendicant orders, then the Jesuits, set out to colonise the Indian imagination in the very domain of visions. Indian visions were reproducing the pictography of the codexes. Yet while the Christian vision was also linked to painting, it was a very different kind of painting, one that was anthropomorphic and dependent on resemblance. On this basis a strategy connecting the image and the vision was organised. Gruzinski[4] points out that the teaching of painting, engraving and sculpture to the Indians and the diffusion of plays inspired by the medieval mysteries showed the status which the mendicant orders had accorded to the image in their evangelical campaigns, thus laying the ground for the visionary experience orchestrated by the Jesuits during the baroque period. The brand of Catholicism which developed close to Mexico, like that of the Andes, was to a large extent an original creation and, in this respect, a reaffirmation of identity. Of course, the type of colonisation, the demographic factors, in short the historical context in broad terms also play a significant part here. But we can say at least that substantial cultural modifications are not incompatible with a strong affirmation of identity.

This is what Georges Balandier pointed out earlier in his commentary on the analyses of S.F. Sundkler.[5] The latter had distinguished two different types of black Church among those set up in reaction to the white Christian presence in South Africa: the type he called 'Sionist' tried to maintain or revive traditional, primarily therapeutic, practices, and affirmed the specificity of African forms of religion. The churches of the 'Ethiopian' type, he noted, were much more marked by Christianity and curtailed their references to tradition. At the same time they were more tolerated by the official authorities, but it was precisely because of this, Balandier observes, that they provided an ideal setting for the formation of the future leaders of Bantu nationalism. In this context, a powerful affirmation of identity was therefore strongly grounded in a substantial cultural change.

Though this does not imply any necessary correlation between cultural change and the affirmation of identity, we must oppose any solidified and frozen representation of identity and culture which would of itself allow them to be seen in total transparency, and again we should bear in mind that both of them are constructions and processes. There is no affirmation of identity without a re-definition of relations of otherness and there is no living culture without cultural creativity. Reference to the past is itself an act of creativity and, one might say, of mobilisation.

What is fascinating about what we shall call, for the sake of brevity, the Jesuit colonisation is that it takes place through the image. Two powerful imaginations confront one another and come together. But they have their confrontation in the realm of practice. The Catholic images are not merely received by the Indians: through painting and sculpture, they undergo adaptation, are re-created and creatively re-made. There emerges a new Indian art which is not to be confused with that of the Spaniards. Today, however, images circulate prodigiously but it is doubtful whether they authorise any re-elaborations comparable to those of the baroque period, since they are received more passively, through screens, and in more solitary conditions.

It is in the nineteenth century in Europe, which prolonged the Enlightenment period and its ideal of modernity, that we have seen the idea of the individual flourish, and likewise, not incompatibly, the respect for local colour which was dear to the romantics and the nationalists. The liberation of peoples and that of individuals were not conceived in contradiction, any more than respect for traditions or local cultures and the idea of progress. In the first poem in his 'Tableaux parisiens', Baudelaire evokes the landscape of Paris wherein co-exist factory chimneys and church bells, the world of tomorrow and that of yesterday which together form that of today. The modern world is a world of accumulation.

None of this can be gainsaid; it is somewhat less simple to aim to foster the individual who is sovereign and autonomous in a 'disenchanted' world and, simultaneously, respect for national and regional diversities. The contradiction erupted in the nineteenth and twentieth centuries in colonial politics which, for example, glorified African cultures, even while reducing them to a kind of folklore and regarding Africans as citizens without full rights, or within national politics which, in France, acknowledged the rights of the citizen for everyone but opposed any overly marked assertion of particularities (regional languages, for example). This contradiction was not to be overcome until, monstrously, the Nazi apocalypse invented both a pure race and a race to be wiped out, mythifying the idea of the individual and projecting it onto the figure of the leader, the *Führer*.

None of the difficulties, none of the fevers of the first half of the twentieth century has entirely disappeared from our horizon. But, even while it is still a difficult business constructing modernity in certain parts of the world, it has been overtaken across the whole surface of the planet by powerful movements of acceleration and excess. The unprecedented development of news media gives us the feeling that history is accelerating. The development of means of transport and com-munication gives us the feeling that the planet is shrinking. And to the extent that each one of us is directly engaged by news information and images, to the extent where the media takes the place of mediations, references become individualised or singularised: to each his own cosmology but to each, also, his own solitude. This movement, which I have proposed calling hyper-modern (in the same way that we talk about things being overdetermined) because it seemed to me to derive from a speeding out of control of the processes which make up modernity,[6] is present everywhere, even if unevenly, even though the areas of hyper-modernity are unequally represented in different countries all over the world. We should further add (and this is what has fuelled Paul Virilio's fears) that it is the very idea of the frontiers of state control that is called into question by hyper-modern acceleration. The logic of some businesses and certain major world centres no longer has anything to do with the national context.

What conclusion are we to reach in terms of our perspective?

After McLuhan, there were some who wanted to see the accelerated development then taking place as prefiguring a global village, with a progressive uniformity modelled on the United States. Others, like our American colleagues in what is known as the 'postmodern' current, insisted, on the contrary, on the breadth of specific cultural claims, and on the cultural polyphony which is now to be heard. In one sense all of them are right, I would say. But one can only measure the breadth of each of these movements by taking into account that they are a part of the same phenomenon – hence the importance of the third criterion of hyper-modernity: individuality, singularity.

Technological development and the globalisation of the colonies can even act against the movement of modernisation operating in some countries, short-circuiting modernity and promoting the emergence of an overdeveloped sector cut off from other components of the local national reality (which are then excluded or at least marginalised) and having direct links with its counterparts in other countries; in other words it can create new frontiers and obliterate others. It can, moreover, foster the circulation of images for passive consumption, a potent factor in collective disintegration and individual alienation. I shall stretch this line of argument a bit further and suggest that one of the great splits in the world today, discernible within urban spaces, is the one whereby poor districts bristling with television aerials stand in contrast to smart districts where satellite dishes blossom: these are not just different temporalities co-existing as in a Baudelairean landscape, but flagrant economic inequalities. Uniformity does not prevent inequality.

The accelerated development of hyper-modernity can only heighten these differences. In parallel, we become inured to images of world catastrophes, of terrorism, mass flight, dead bodies: a spectacle made abstract by force of familiarity. Yet it sometimes happens that an adept media strategy can serve the cause of those whom one would instead readily imagine to be its victims. This was how the Chiapas guerrillas in Mexico – dubbed by some as the first postmodern guerrillas – were able to make themselves internationally known and simultaneously play a significant national role thanks to their publicist's 'communication skills'.

The image can have all kinds of uses. It can also be a staging post for all kinds of extremist reactions to hyper-modernity. It is well known that the Algerian fundamentalists have given a nickname to the satellite dishes which enable their compatriots to keep the outside world in view; they call these *antennes paraboliques 'antennes paradiaboliques'*, in other words, 'devil's dishes'. But this demonisation does not prevent the Islamic movements, like others, from acquiring television channels or Internet sites in order to put forward claims to other forms of universality. If hyper-modernity can have the effect of dissolving or abstracting the figure of the other (which is the best way of breaking the dynamic of the identity/alterity pairing), the reactions which it provokes and relays can be equally totalising, excluding and alienating. Specificities on the one hand, fundamentalism and zealotry on the other, share alike in what Georges Devereux called 'support' or 'class' identities, in the logical rather than the sociological meaning of the term. In the development of these collective and exclusive identities Devereux saw the signs of an imminent collapse of individual identity.[7]

Thus we are afforded one fixed point of reference: so long as the identity/alterity dialectic functions, the assertion of belonging to a collectivity cannot be conceived either as exclusive of other affiliations nor as exclusive of the assertion of individual identity. But this dialectic is curbed as much by the effects of dissolution which can be imputed to hyper-modern technologies, as by the effects of hardening and freezing induced by the withdrawal into exclusive affiliations. When the relationship to the world becomes congealed or virtualised, it removes identity from the test of alterity. It thus creates the conditions for solitude and is likely to engender an I that is just as artificial as the image it devises of others.

WHAT IS AT STAKE
DREAM, MYTH, FICTION

THE AMBIGUITIES OF THE DREAM

Individuals have always had trouble identifying with anything other than the body, always being tempted instead to think of it as a boundary to be breached or defended. This uneasy understanding of the body as a somewhat porous frontier does not inherently imply any dualistic conception opposing body and spirit. In Africa, for example, the element of the personality which escapes from the body during night time dreaming is regarded as a part of it, most usually in terms of the vital principle, a principle which is possibly distinct from the one which reproduces and transmits the image of the body or again from the one which contains and retains the most individual part of the individual. To take one among sundry examples: among the Nupe, B.G.M. Nadel[1] identifies the *rayi*, the vital principle, the *life soul*, in Latin the *anima,* which is present in all living beings but is to some extent separate since it is this, during dreaming, which frees itself from the body's boundaries and goes wandering: what an individual sees in his or her dream is what the *rayi* sees in the course of its roaming around. But the *rayi* cannot travel alone; it is accompanied by the *fifingi*, which is the double and the image of the individual body. It is the *fifingi* which is seen by those who dream about him through the intermediary of their *rayi*. The double is bound

26

to the living body: it is the shadow it casts. It survives death and continues to make appearances in the dreams of the living, even though individual identity, be it of someone living or dead, corresponds to another entity: the *kuci*. It is to the *kuci* of someone recently dead or to that of an ancestor that sacrifices are made in order to ward off what is regarded as a bad dream, according to the Nupe key to dreams.

What all the African systems of representation stage, through what are obviously different instances (I'm thinking principally of the Dogon, the Bambara, the Mossi, the Tallensi, the Ashanti, the Anyi or Ivory Coast lagoon peoples, the Ewe, the Ibo and the Yoruba, for which we have a vast literature at our disposal) is the reality of the dream (to be more precise, the continuity between waking life and the life of the dream), the plurality of the self (despite the presence of an inherently elusive element in which is expressed the most individual part of the individual) and what one could call the material intimacy between the body and the elements which inhabit it, which leave it and come back to it. The body on waking experiences all the weariness of the journey travelled by its double. The body of the newborn carries the mark of the ancestral element which is reincarnated within it.

The dream, we can see, entails a double movement, of exit and return, of one or several of the elements which make up the personality. Without this return the life of the dreamer is at stake and the whole process of the dream is in question. Even if we confine ourselves to their most current definitions, dream and possession would therefore be inverse rather than opposed phenomena.

Shamanism and possession have, however, often been set against one another as opposites. It is 'the direction of the movement connecting man and the spirit world' which then needs to be brought in since 'shamanism is man rising towards the gods', as Jean Pouillon[2] reminds us, while Luc de Heusch[3] tells us that 'possession is a "descent" of the gods and an incarnation'. We can easily see the movements in inverse direction which are being indicated here. But we can also observe, by making reference to the body of the shaman or the person possessed, that the two phenomena are defined by a single absence: the absence of their own bodies, both for the journeying shaman, who abandons it, and the possessed one, who is dispossessed and excluded from it.

All we have to do now is ask some questions about the nature of this journey undertaken and this exclusion. The dream (and not just the shamanic dream) is clearly described and most often understood as a journey but, by the same token, it exists only through the story of which it is the object – the dream narrative, the first traveller's tale. The dream narrated, the story of the dream, defines a relation to three terms: the dreamer-narrator on the one hand, the listener on the other, with the status of the third term remaining uncertain by virtue of the effects of displacement and condensation which are peculiar to oneiric activity (I dream of myself, but is it myself? Of an other, but which one? Is it another?). The dreamer is the author of his dream but the dream imposes an image of himself and of his relation to others which he might reject in his waking state. The dream introduces a problematic relation between oneself and one's self. The third term of the dream (its subject) is enigmatic and this enigma can be submitted to those who specialise in interpretation.

Possession is not the story of an event but is itself event and advent. It is the object of a performance and it is acted out, in the theatrical sense of the term. The acting of the possessed person is strictly contemporaneous with the coming of the power which possesses him or her. Nonetheless the possessed person is dispossessed of herself or himself. Through her mouth – but not through her voice, which is transformed and made unrecognisable – it is someone else who expresses her and

addresses her to others than herself, even if the latter make up
a collectivity of which she is part: in relation to them, her
possessed body is now no more than a mediation or a medium.
The part she plays, the character whom she mimes are, at the
moment of possession, asserted as the truth of an appearance
which is modelled with some degree of stress on the stereotype
of the power which is incarnated. What now becomes
important is no longer memory and the problematic relation
of oneself to one's self. On the contrary once the person
possessed is no longer possessed, she must forget not that she
has been so (possessions are often programmed like theatrical
performances or parties) but in what conditions she has been
so. The return to oneself (after the departure of the possessing
and overlapping power) is often enacted in an overstated
manner. Thus in the sessions held by the Brazilian Umbanda
we can see young women rubbing their eyes, shaking their
heads and stretching to make it quite clear that the *caboclo*
which possessed them is gone and that they are having trouble
recovering their spirits, knowing where they are and what has
happened to them, even though their performance, while the
caboclo was imposing the rhythm and appearances of its
possession, was greeted by prolonged applause. The quality of
the acting is thereby recognised but it is recognised for what
it is: the sign of a full and genuine possession, of which there
must be no awareness on the part of the person expressing it.

What happens during the dream is played out on waking,
when it is subjected to the triple constraints of memory,
narrative and interpretation. And it is the last of these that most
often concerns the dreamer himself, even when it raises
questions about those close to him.[4] The relationship enacted
between the dreamer and the interpreter is a private and unique
one. What happens during possession is played out contem-
poraneously with the advent-event itself, through the speech
of a power which addresses itself to others (possibly to admonish

or encourage them) about which the person possessed is supposed to have had no awareness and *a fortiori* to have no recollection when, in a very literal sense, he comes back to himself. Possession that is unconscious but played out in the theatrical meaning of the expression, also therefore defines a relation to three terms: the possessing power, the spectators or witnesses and the person possessed. The last of these, dispossessed of himself or, to be more precise, of his body, is not enigmatic but absent. To be more precise, we could contrast an *enigma of presence* (of the dreamer towards his or her dream) with an *enigma of absence* (of the possessed person towards the possession whose object he or she is).

In each of these relations which defines, respectively, the dream and the possession, the third term is therefore always problematic.

The dreamer-narrator is to some extent the spectator of a reconstituted dream: his or her connection with the 'events' of a dream is apparently passive (we mark this with a minus sign in the table that follows), even if we know that in the plot of the dream something of him, someone whom he identifies as himself, seems to play an important part (we therefore correct the minus sign with a plus sign which we shall subordinate to it: ±). As for the possessed person, he or she is an actor. Everything in his manifest behaviour indicates a series of actions which can reach the point of violence and which are intended for the eyes of a spectator (+). But these actions, we're told, are not his. With regard to himself he is absent (−) and the possession, on the whole, in terms of the possessed person's role, is presented as combining the hyperactivity of a body with the assumed absence of the person who inhabits it (±). In relation to the scenario of the dream and the spectacle of the possession, the dreamer and the possessed person are simultaneously active and passive, authors and non-authors, but from this standpoint their respective positions can be regarded as symmetrical and reversed: the dream is imposed on the one who is its author and the possession is acted out by the one who undergoes it.

The one who is privileged to hear the dream is the specialist in its interpretation (the soothsayer, the augur, the psychoanalyst). Called as a witness, this specialist plays an active role (+) through his contribution to the clarification of an individual enigma. By contrast, the spectators of the possession play no part in it (−), even if the possessed person happens to be surrounded by a number of assistants who keep check on his or her performance. For example, the possessions I witnessed in Togoland, in the Anfouin region, among the Goun and Mina, were often violent and the women in a trance were taken away after a time and calmed down by the cult leader's assistants. In some cases, the spectators are even the intended recipients of the message delivered by the possessing power through the mouth of the person possessed.

As for characters who are dreamt or embodied, we must discuss them in terms of identity rather than role, because their role depends on the recognition of their identity. Even if they wear familiar countenances, the characters in the dream have an identity which at the very least is fluid and elusive, and, on waking, if he is attentive enough to remember, the dreamer will find himself faced with the enigma of his own image (−). On the stage of the possession, the symbolic is explicitly social: the possessing powers are listed and described (+). In the case of Togo and the Benin Gulf region in general these are evoked like the characteristic personnel of the mythic repertoire, playing an active part in a veritable pantheon. No enigma here: for the spectators this is merely a socially coded event, merely a matter of recognising the power incarnated in a male or female body. A mask can be a help, in certain cults, and the spoken word which is then to be heard through it is normative or prescriptive. It does not question the social order, as the soothsayer questions the individual dream, but itemises it in order to maintain or restore it.

Table 1

Categories Agents	Dream	Possession
Authors	$\mp$	$\pm$
Witnesses	$+$	$-$
Characters	$-$	$+$

On the basis of these two symmetrical and reversed figures we can now pinpoint and reformulate the enigma of the third term. It derives in fact from the tension exerted over the terms of a dual relation (dreamer/listener in one case, possessed/possessor in the other) to suggest the existence of a third term and of a compound relation. The dreamer's narrative suggests to the listener the existence of a dreamed subject (a subject nonetheless to the degree in which it acts in the dream) and the spectacle of the possessed body suggests to the spectators the existence of a possessing subject. What is in question in the former case is the relation of the dreamer to the dreamed, in other words a relation of self to self where the second 'self' is tainted with alterity, and what is in question in the latter is the relation of the possessed person to the possessor, in other words a relation of self to another, but to another tainted with identity. For the dreamed subject who acts in the dream is not fully identical to the dreamer (to the dreaming subject) and the possessing power is not completely alien to the person who is possessed (a return will be made). Nor is it totally alien to the spectator to the degree that, in systems where possessing powers are clearly distinguished, the spectator recognises and locates it in relation to other figures of possession.

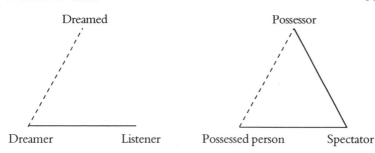

That said, the 'enigma of the third term', which can take several forms, is not necessarily bound to an opposition between dream and possession of the type represented in Table 1. The latter projection is only possible within a combination whose terms can be switched around, should one replace the excessively generalised concepts of 'dream' and 'possession' with local concepts which are never the strict equivalent. 'Dream' and 'possession' thus allow themselves to be decomposed into a certain number of intermediary figures which, far from being in opposition, arise rather from a series of transformations.[5]

Let us go back to the example of the Pumé-Yaruro and their shaman-singer. Gemma Orobitg[6] shows that their oneiric categories are three in number. *Handikia* designate all the forms of 'dream' (the waking dream of the *cantador* as well as the sleeping dream) which allow the dreamer-traveller to go far away, into the world of the gods or the dead; this category therefore essentially distinguishes the world of distant powers from the terrestrial world nearby, one landscape from another. *Kanehe* designates the sleeping dream, to the exclusion of all forms of waking vision. *Handivaga* is distinguished from the first two categories and is applied to the forms of waking vision which, however, are close at hand (hallucinations, ghosts). On the occasion of the ceremony of the *tohe* these diverse forms are put into operation. As we have seen, the shaman, or rather one of his *pumetho*, travels the distant world of the gods and the dead but he does not sleep; we see him singing and smoking fat cigars while another of his *pumetho* welcomes one or other divine power, one or other ancestor or more recent member of the dead as they visit living men. The assistants who accompany the song of the shaman all night long, and who, like him, smoke a great deal of tobacco and inhale *yopo*, a hallucinogenic preparation which is widespread among all the Indian groups in the region, stay awake as long as they can, but the forms of hallucination (*handivaga*) connected with fatigue or a moment's lapse into sleep are not uncommon.

As for the shaman's 'journey', one could define it, in at least two senses, as a 'place-between-dreams'. The great shaman of Riecito, the village where Gemma Orobitg worked, told her in confidence that when he agreed to lead the *tohe*, to be its shaman-traveller, it was after he had been invited to do so by the divine powers during the dream as he slept. Moreover this shaman preferred often to sleep before recounting his journey (his waking 'dream'). This new sleeping dream, which fell into the categories of both *handikia* and *kanehe*) enabled him to confirm and to detail − on the basis of the encounters he experienced in it − his visions and the adventures that have occurred during the waking dream which, for its part, fell into the single category of *handikia*. There is more: the arrival of the gods among men in the course of the *tohe* ceremony (the form of 'vocal possession' mentioned a little earlier) is sometimes presented as a dream of the gods (*handikia*), as if the union of gods and men stemmed from the fact that they 'dream' about one another reciprocally. The *tohe*, which takes place in the eyes of the shaman as something between an annunciation dream and a confirmation dream, can therefore also be regarded as the intersection point of the dream of men and the dream of gods.

Let us add that, in this example, the 'dream' (or, to be more precise, the different Pumé oneiric categories) and the 'possession', far from being in opposition, are conditional one on the other, since it is while the shaman is 'travelling' (in other words at the point when one of the *pumetho*, an essential component of his being, leaves the corporeal envelope) that the divine power is said to come close to him. Moreover, there are at least two forms of 'possession'. Possession strictly speaking, if by this we mean total investment of body and being, to the point where it is substantially conveyed by a total alteration in the voice, is rare. Most often, the divine power is said to take up position above the head of the shaman and to communicate to him an energy which resonates in the quality of his singing, which is to say simultaneously in the timbre of the voice, the rhythm of the musical phrasing and the potency of its subject. For the shaman always improvises his singing, even if there are very definite fixed musical forms and even if the text concerns the approach and the arrival of gods. The assertion whereby it is the gods who begin to sing in the middle of the night when everything is as it should be, suggests not so much a substitution as a fulfilment and a form of perfection, a momentary trans-formation of human song.

If we go back to Table 1 and we replace the undifferenti-ated categories of 'dream' and 'possession' with the Pumé categories, we see a new configuration taking shape. The 'dreamer' (if we think of the shaman's waking dream possibly as induced by the taking of a hallucinogenic and interpreted by the sleeping dream) is presented as very obviously active (+): he enters into discussion with the gods and confronts them in order to rescue the *pumetho* of the sick and the dying whom they have stolen away for one reason or another. The 'possessed' person for his part is only half active: he welcomes the arrival of the gods without being entirely invested by them but, at the crucial moment, it is the voice of the gods that one seems to hear. The more active role is therefore that of the travelling *pumetho* (regarded moreover as the more important), that of the *pumetho* who is present at the *tohe* being more passive (−). One cannot, however, fail to acknowledge the quality of the *cantador's* performance − which is even more spectacular in certain forms of *tohe* that subject the shaman to running in circles for an entire part of the night, accompanied by his assistants, in order to represent the journey of his first *pumetho*. But it is really because, in this form of *tohe*, the shaman also plays his part as a dreamer that his activity appears the more active. As a whole, in the conception that one forms of the shaman as dreamer-traveller and singer-possessed person, the role of the singer-possessed person cannot be considered as merely passive (∓).

In the case of listeners and spectators, the relationship is likewise modified. Among the Pumé there is no specialised function of dream interpreter (−) and, if any need for it is felt, the shaman-traveller recounts and himself interprets the vagaries of his journey − whose outcome interests others beside himself whenever he goes off on a search for the *pumetho* of sick individuals. The participants in the *tohe*, for their part, play an important role since the *cantador* needs their responses and needs the choir, which is made up primarily of women and girls alongside the men. But this role remains secondary (∓) in relation to that of the shaman himself, which we have just made clear was more actively that of dreamer (far from the scene of the *tohe*) than of, to all intents and purposes, a person possessed.

When it comes to the characters of the 'dream' and the 'possession', be they gods or the dead, they pose a particular problem. On the one hand they are very specifically identified and the collective symbolic seems to have so strongly imprinted the Pumé imagination that one frequently finds reference to the Pumé divinities in the narrations of sleeping dreams. The coming of the gods, like that of the dead, during sleep, as during the *tohe*, poses no problem of identity (+ in both cases). But, if one takes a historical perspective and focuses attention on the contemporary situation, one will be aware of a significant alteration: in their pictured and topographic language, the Pumé say that the most ancient gods have gone far away, and that the most accessible areas of their world are now only frequented by new gods. They say too, referring to the *tohe* ceremony, that the gods 'come down' less and less often; the last god to make occasional descents was Ishi Ai, a kind of local Hermes, a specialist in mediation, from which we understand that he is one of the most faithful to the men/gods connection. Probably it is the threat of their own extinction which the Pumé are bringing to mind when they talk about the growing remoteness of the gods. The classic problem of the dream (Who is it I am dreaming about?) is thus transposed onto possession (Is the being who comes down to me really there?). The history of the century shifts the mystery of presence from the dream to possession.

In Table 2, therefore, we shall differentiate 'characters' in terms of the anthropological standpoint: (a), always re-asserted locally, which means that there is no question over the identity of the characters met on the scene of the dream and of the *tohe*, and the historical standpoint (b) which must take into account the fact that these characters themselves have changed over the last 50 or 60 years, as is borne out by the literature of the years between 1930 and 1940, and that some of the most prestigious among them are by now inaccessible – remote like memories which the younger generations have already missed out on.

What the Pumé diagram adds to the general diagram of the formal opposition between dream and possession, which firmly defines the shaman as a singer-composer-improviser, is the component of inspiration, in the literary and artistic meaning of the term. In inspiration, the role of the author is simultaneously active and passive ($\mp$). Everything comes from somewhere else (from a god, from a Muse), but at the cost of intense work (inspiration has to be found). As for the listener, if he or she is able to interpret the work and respond to it, he is in the first place its receiver (∓).

Table 2

Categories Agents	Handikia Kanehe	Tohe
Authors	+	∓
Witnesses	−	∓
Characters a)	+	+
b)	−	−

Any ethnological attempt to understand the nature of 'dream' and 'possession' in diverse populations is necessarily based on an acknowledgement of the inner plurality of the person (of the ' self ') whose local conceptions of oneiric or hallucinatory phenomena, in their diversity, are no more than specific illustrations. We should bear in mind here that there are convergences at several points with pagan representations − convergences which indeed would allow us to subsume them under a single concept such as paganism. These convergences are not just formal, they have a content; they correspond to propositions or hypotheses which merit discussion, and these are of interest to us on the one hand in the same terms as any proposition of a philosophical order, and on the other, because they are formative of the symbolic bonds which join individuals together in society. Of course, this is not about sorting out truth from error. This was something that the Church got involved in when it undertook to root out paganism, for example by making a distinction between the two 'dream gates' − the dream as illusion and the dream as premonition. But because it is something which responds to a necessity that Jacques Le Goff highlighted by stressing the way in which all social life has an imaginary component, the assessment of this ensemble of propositions and hypotheses can enlighten us about the functioning of symbolic activity, which is to say all activity of a kind that shapes the necessary bonds between the same and the other, between identity and alterity.

On at least three points (the plurality of the self, the non-dualistic conception of the real, the interpretation of the event as a sign and incidentally of the dream as an event) African, Amerindian, Oceanian and other cosmologies provide us with room to reflect on the precise extent to which, whether it be as anthropologies or cosmologies, they correspond to hypotheses which focus on the nature of individual reality and relations between individuals.

The topic of the plurality of the self, which we have confronted from the outset, is one which can be broken down and it is worth examining in detail. But the topics of non-dualism and the event-sign are preliminary to this examination. Conceptions of the multiple self do not set physical against mental, material against spiritual or corporeal against psychic. In order to imagine the kind of representations associated with them, we only have to make an effort to take literally some of the expressions which we currently use such as 'to have guts', 'to have lost one's head', 'to be beside oneself', 'to have the stomach' or 'to lack the stomach' for something.

Nor is there any dualism in the conception of the relationships between gods and men. Both in dream and in possession men are dealing with powers of a different order from themselves but not of a different nature. From the moment when they are individualised and singularised (objects, in a sense, of a work of supplementary symbolisation in relation to pure, diffuse forces and energies, which are identified with a receptacle that is simultaneously specific and reproducible, with a 'fetish', but which nonetheless lack the form and status of a person), those beings which for the sake of convenience we call 'gods' are usually presented by mythologies as ancient men or, at the very least, beings who in ancient times lived on earth. In a pantheon as developed as that of the former Dahomey, there is no doubt about the human origin of the great divinities. In one of the Ivory Coast prophet-healers, Koudou Jeannot, whose return to paganism over the last few years had the status of a quite extraordinary occurrence (in as much as it amounted to an openly stated political opposition to the Ivory Coast authorities), through Jean-Pierre Dozon, we have witnessed the establishment of a cult of fertility. The prophet's brother, who died at the start of the 1980s, was buried close to the village; then, under the name of Gbahie, he became the main driver of the cult, which is now very popular. An altar was built at the foot of a tree whose roots appeared to grow out of his tomb. In the eyes of an uninformed observer, the ritual developed by the prophet, who now eliminates all Christian references from his message, could not be distinguished from those which it is possible to see taking place in countries where the pagan tradition is preserved, such as Togoland or Benin. With Koudou Jeannot we have certainly witnessed the birth of a god.[7]

During the journey of his *pumetho*, the Pumé shaman encounters gods and the *pumetho* of human beings some of whom are the dead, and others merely sick on earth (by the very fact that their *pumetho* has been displaced among the gods). During the *tohe*, not only can the gods of the pantheon make an appearance, but also ancestors or the more recent dead. Thus, during the *tohe* one of my interlocutors had been pleased to receive 'live' news from his uncle who had died a few weeks earlier. The mythological powers are designated by the term '*nibe*', which literally means 'those from outside', a term which is applied more widely to all of those who come from other places, and above all to the whites. The terminology, the status of the dead, the narratives of cosmogony and the weaving together of the different worlds, which are all set in motion in the individual and collective imagination by the ceremony of the *tohe*, postulate a common nature between gods and men. Men are the past of the gods, the gods are the future of men, in an earthly world which it can be feared, quite plainly, will be without a future for those who more than ever are condemned by the harshness of the times to death and dream.

When I was with the Alladians in the 1960s, my informants had no hesitation in using the term 'double life', when they tried to give me some idea of the nocturnal perambulations of one of the governing principles of the *wawi,* the person who, with relative autonomy, undergoes certain experiences of which the dream, if ever it was remembered on waking, was the vague and problematic residue. The *wawi* himself, in his aggressive guise (*awa*), was called to account in the interpretation of all unlucky events. This interpretation itself naturally made a abstraction of the waking/sleeping divide, which has no pertinence in terms of what one could call an *episteme* of immanence. Under the influence of Catholic missionaries, various Protestant Churches and, finally, of local prophets, who cleverly strove to modify the spirit of the faith by subverting the letter of it, the Alladians also spoke in terms of a 'devil life'. In relation to this one might recall the extraordinary ethnographic intuition which Maupassant displays in his novella *Le Horla*, which, the other way round, conjures the hallucinations provoked by a passing Brazilian ship freighted with exotic powers, in a first-person hero haunted by the invading presence of a force whose identity is unknown to him but which he foresees means to enter into him and take his place.

If the narration and the analysis of the dream are so important, most of the time it is not so much because the dream represents ey, the expression or the projection of waking life, as because it is both the anticipation and the sequel to an experience which is undergone also in the waking state. The vagaries of the dream and those of the waking state ceaselessly perform a mutual interpretation. Thus, a young man on the Ivory Coast, facing accusations before a prophet–healer of the lagoon region, confesses that he ate human flesh and then explains that in a dream he obeyed the suggestion of a stranger offering him a piece of meat whose true nature was unknown to him; one young Pumé woman confided in Gemma Orobitg, whom she trusted, that she was afraid of being pregnant by a man other than her husband because she had dreamt of committing adultery. The events of the dream are useful for interpreting observations made in the waking state (a swollen belly, the absence of periods) but they are not so much signs as antecedents or causes. Paradoxically, the value of sign could be given rather to the event of the waking state (an illness for example) – but solely because it refers back to an earlier event. The latter, whether it is dreamt or otherwise, most usually implicates some part or other of a human individual (either as victim or aggressor).

The ambiguity of the dreams studied by ethnologists therefore depends overall on a number of complementary factors: the continuity between waking and the dream; the multiplicity of oneiric forms, which is not reducible to the waking/sleeping opposition; the plurality of the self: the one held responsible for a crime committed as a double is neither entirely guilty (it was a part of him that acted 'as a double'), nor entirely innocent (it was indeed 'he' who acted). He is responsible but not guilty: as long as 30 years ago this formula struck me as being quite applicable to the way in which those accused of witchcraft in equatorial African societies were regarded during their trials. Moreover, the plurality of the self gives shape to the ambivalence of feelings. If those accused of witchcraft are so easily convinced of the reality of their crimes, it is because underlying their dreams there are real discords and tensions. It is perhaps also because there is no individual order that can make an abstraction of a more collective order and that, for many, it is better to be condemned (but in a reinstating sense) than excluded. It is because the dream is revelatory (of disharmonies in the social fabric and in the fever for order) that it can so easily be inscribed within the logical and experienced continuity of life.

ASSESSING THE PLURALITY OF THE SELF

We have seen that the discriminatory criterion for possession and its related forms was the oblivion which they had to undergo, which they could not but undergo, while the dream existed only through the memory that was kept of it. It is therefore not surprising that, in the cultures where they co-exist, dream and possession affect different instances of the human person – as in the case of the Pumé where the *pumetho* travelling in dream is not the same *pumetho* who greets the divine powers, simultaneously, in the *tohe.*

But, beyond any opposition between dream and possession, memory and forgetting, or unconscious and conscious, there are two distinct conceptions of the plurality of the self which are brought into play. The first of these is alternative, and can be compared with the theme of multiple personality which is currently fashionable in the United States. Taken to its extreme, this model offers us a series of different personalities who can, according to circumstances, within a heavily symbolised system, or by some uncontrollable arbiter – in the case of individual pathology – be substituted one for the other, each of them constituting a complete personality with its own name besides. There is a second notion which is instead aggregational. It is especially exemplified in the African systems for which the individual is merely the ephemeral collection of elements of diverse origins, some of which pre-existed at his or her birth and will survive his or her death in different combinations defining other individualities. Some of the rituals celebrated at birth are intended to identify them more precisely by connecting them either to precise social and symbolic aspects, or to more aleatory elements such as the day and circumstance of the birth or else the primordial sign which is established by the casting of kola nuts or cowrie shells. Obviously, even more care is taken (and manipulation is likely to be exercised) over pinpointing these elements in the case of kingdoms where descent, heredity, inheritance and succession must signify the fundamental unity of a dynasty. This was how in the former Fon kingdom of Dahomey specialists recognised in the person of each sovereign the fundamental principle (known as the *joto*) which, very literally, identified a part of him with one of his predecessors and ancestors. The dynastic chain was therefore defined not just through the agnatic line of succession of individuals who were related but further through the intertwining of two or three lines of identity around the genealogical tree.

One can easily see how the first notion fits the model of possession. The personality which is expressed through the possessed body is quite plainly one that is different from its habitual inhabitant. This at least is the postulate: during the Umbanda sessions at which I was able to be present in Belém, in Brazil, after the dances and the trance state were over, at the point when the possessed persons were not yet, however, officially released from their borrowed identity, it was common to hear them speak in bland everyday conversational terms about themselves, but in the third person: 'My horse has problems with her daughter who is doing badly at school ... .' Conversely, people know in Africa just as they do in America that it is not a good idea to wake someone up suddenly; if the dreaming authority has not resumed its place alongside others then it is the whole person who can be stricken with madness or die. The Alladians made very clear the need for the perfect knitting together of the two principal authorities of the personality (the travelling and connective *wawi* and the *ee*, the stable and vital element) by explaining that one of the most common misdeeds of the witchdoctors was to tug at one of them; the result of the slight discrepancy brought about in this way was a dizziness and a fever which could lead to loss of consciousness and to death. In these terms, the plurality of the self can be understood only as something fully governed and integrated.

Paradoxically, the aggregational mode is undoubtedly the most representative in Africa, in societies where possession plays an institutional role, whereas among the Amerindians, who attach a primordial significance to the dream, the alternative mode is most common. In actual fact, the tension between the alternative (or substitutional) notion and the cumulative (integrational) notion of the self is internal to all notions of the person. More precisely, the concern to define the individual as *one,* which is expressed in relation to the dream, when reference is made to the absolute necessity for the wandering authority to return to the body of the dreamer (even the Pumé shaman insists upon this necessity and recognises the overwhelming role of the travelling *pumetho,* even while he gives a meaning and attributes a personality to each of his other *pumethos*), is a concern encountered, in relation to possession, with the insistence upon the specific bond linking the possessing power to the individual who is possessed. Everything takes place as if, far from estranging him or her from some external personality, possession confers an extra identity upon the person it touches.

How does this apparent reversal work? The accounts and
analyses of Michel Leiris in *La Possession et ses aspects théâtraux
chez les Éthiopiens de Gondar*[8] give us quite a clear idea. Let us
first of all remember that, if we accept what Leiris says, among
the Ethiopians of Gondar it was an illness, an accident or a
personality disturbance which gave rise to the assumption of
an attack by a *zar* spirit, and which triggered the trajectory that,
with the initiation concluded, was to turn the sufferer and
former sick person into a regular and recognised possessed
person. Some of the *zars* (particularly those of the healer) were
transmitted by inheritance. Without going any further into the
detail of a very rich and very subtle account, let us still bear in
mind that possession in Gondar was clearly presented as a series
of incarnations by very pre-established powers, obliging the
possessed person to act out various made-up roles. Let us finally
bear in mind that, in a very classic sense, the fit of possession
had to be forgotten:

> Whenever anyone (be it a healer or a follower) has been possessed
> by a *zar* and has returned to their normal state or become possessed
> by a different *zar*, it is the custom that they behave as if they had
> retained no memory of this phase which is now over, and which
> corresponds to a fit that they are supposed not even to have been
> conscious of.[9]

The question which is now long since overlaid on this type of
account concerns the good or bad faith of the possessed persons.
The beginning of an answer is furnished by Leiris or rather by
two sayings that he brings to us, which are indeed very
interesting: 'A *zar* resembles its horse', and then, 'Like horse,
like *zar*.'[10] These sayings invert the order of resemblances: it
is no longer the possessed person who replicates the outline
and the character of the possessing power but the latter who
resembles the possessed person. Leiris moreover draws our

attention to the fact that, among the numerous spirits who can possess a single individual, the only ones who really matter are those which have been attached to him or her in accordance with custom and with priority given to the one which was first attributed to him, and to which he will always be very close. The *zar* which resembles its horse therefore reinforces the personality of the possessed person rather than replacing it, and this makes it clear at once why the name of the *zar* which is cleverly devolved to the 'sufferer' at the time of initiation will constitute for him or her in the long run a kind of civil status or passport. The question of good or bad faith is thus bypassed. And in the ordinary course of everyday life (outside the times of ritual) the specific relationship with a particular *zar* is brought up to justify a change of mood or a decision: the *zar* becomes the equivalent of a personal character trait and the one afflicted by it can deplore it while at the same time referring to it by way of apology.

This brings us more than ever into the episteme of immanence. Leiris does in fact observe that certain *zars* are regarded as 'historically defined human stock'[11] and that *zars* in general constantly intervene in everyday life; as a result they are considered as being 'at the root of certain human events whose heroes they will be regarded as and which may well be integrated into their myth'.[12] This spectacular 'return to sender', as one might call it, very obviously reveals the extent of the closeness between men and *zars* and the way in which the myth is fuelled by human history.

Leiris raises a final point which seems to me to be very bound up with the question of personality. The question is whether possession in the strict sense may be construed as the result of an action being effected from the outside, of a domination rather than a penetration and inner habitation. After studying the vocabulary of possession, the ethnologist is inclined to think that the first of these hypotheses is very much the right one. He takes this a little further still and wonders whether the possessed person is really plunged into a state of unawareness at the time of the possession. The question would be of only relative interest were there not also the issue of the personality of the possessed person – his or her identity, and not his or her sincerity. But the fact is that when it comes to the confession made to Leiris by one of the practitioners of possession, it is less important for us to uncover its contradictions (for example, he discloses that the loss of consciousness is at least progressive, and when he speaks in the first person, he confesses to the pleasure which is prompted in him by the fact of becoming transformed into a *zar* as the *zar* is being transformed into a man, into an Amhara) than to locate in it the tension of identity which makes any wholly alternative notion of personality impossible.

It was this very impossibility, as I have mentioned in *Le Dieu objet*, that was stressed by one of Bernard Maupoil's informants when he confided to him, regarding possession in the lands of the Fon, that the *voodoo* do not fall upon their followers but that they 'go to their heads': 'your voodoo is in your own bones. Life does not whisper in a person's ear: it is in your very bones that it speaks.'[13] The fact that there is the other in the same (that the personality is always threatened by an eruption of its different component parts) is to some extent balanced by the evidence the other way round, by knowing that there is the same in the other and that the powers which invest the 'possessed person' resemble him or were already present in him as potentiality.

THE THREE AXES OF THE IMAGINARY

On dark nights or clear ones in the Pumé land, beneath the flimsy covering of a roof made of leaves, sometimes of sheet metal, or in the open air, under the starry sky which slowly swings from east to west, everyone asleep can live out their own dreaming, or with others listen until dawn to the shaman improvising his song and calling up their shared mythology, the myth that always re-begins. The individual dream, freighted with the residues of everyday, with fantasies and mythic images; the myth, re-worked and enriched by the waking dream of the familiar from other worlds; and the song, which draws the gods, seduces them and captures them for a moment, as if they obeyed the injunction of mortal beings. These are the three axes of a differentiated imaginary which circulates between each of them and nourishes itself on each one of them. Human beings need the song and the shaman so that they can hear the gods and believe in their dreams, and the shaman needs to dream so that he can believe in his song and his journey.

In our own tradition, the subtle link that runs from the dream to the myth and to the literary or artistic work was one of Freud's objects of investigation. In the first place he was interested in the relationship between 'day-dreaming' and 'creative writing'. Both, he stated, were 'a continuation of, and a substitute for, what was once the play of childhood'. These words have a certain significance here, and so therefore does their translation into French. This statement of Freud's is taken from an article, 'Creative Writers and Day-Dreaming', originally published in 1908 in the Berlin *Neue Revue* with the title 'Der Dichter und das Phantasieren'.[14] The day-dream or waking dream is the 'fantasy' (in French *fantaisie*), which is usually translated within psychoanalysis as 'phantasy' (*fantasme*). In German it is expressed as '*phantasieren*', substantifying the verb, which better expresses the action of phantasying, of producing phantasies or phantasms. As for the expression 'creative writer' (*créateur littéraire*), it aims to render the sense of '*Dichter*' – which does not exclusively designate poet in the technical meaning of the term but the creator in a wider sense.

The child at play, Freud tells us, behaves like a creative writer, 'in that he creates a world of his own, or, rather, rearranges the things of his world in a new way which pleases him'. But he distinguishes his world of play quite well from reality, 'and he likes to link his imagined objects and situations to the tangible and visible things of the real world'.[15] The opposite of play is reality, but play, which is distinguished from it, is not entirely detached from it. In a sense, the creative writer does the same as the child at play: he takes his world of phantasy seriously but he separates it sharply from reality. The result of this is that 'many things which, if they were real, could give no enjoyment, can do so in the play of phantasy, and many excitements which, in themselves, are actually distressing, can become a source of pleasure for the hearers and spectators at the performance of a writer's work'.[16]

Instead of playing, the growing child *phantasies*. He gives up 'the link with real objects' which belonged to play. He becomes a day-dreamer: 'He ... creates what are called *day-dreams*.'[17] Phantasy is a 'correction of unsatisfying reality'; it does not play with it but escapes from it; it finds in the present an occasion for awakening hidden desires, for giving fresh life to memories and projecting a dreamed of situation into the future. If phantasies become over-powerful, 'the conditions are laid for an onset of neurosis or psychosis'.[18] But at some time or another everyone construct phantasies, and day-dreams, like night-time dreams, are primarily the fulfilment of wishes.

The child's play is therefore the source of the phantasy which is its substitute and of the creative work which continues it. But creative work is in itself a mystery. A mystery for the author, at least for the author of the psychological novels which Freud has in mind in his essay, who is inclined 'to split up his ego, by self-observation, into many part-egos, and, in consequence, to personify the conflicting currents of his own mental life in several heroes'[19] (thus one could sketch out an additional resemblance between the shaman who creates songs and the author with multiple personalities). A mystery all the more so for the reader, since, Freud tells us, while the phantasies of others repel us or at least leave us cold, they can give us great pleasure when they are presented in a literary form. Freud looks for explanations for this paradox. He believes that 'the essential *ars poetica* lies in the technique of overcoming the feeling of repulsion in us which is undoubtedly connected with the barriers that rise between each single ego and the others'. The writer 'softens the character of his egoistic day-dreams by altering and disguising it' and he gives the reader a 'yield of pleasure', enabling 'the release of still greater pleasure arising from deeper psychical sources'. Freud gives this yield of pleasure a special name: '*incentive bonus* or *fore-pleasure*', and he attributes it to 'a liberation of tensions in our minds', while he concludes by suggesting that perhaps some of this effect is due to the writer's example, which enables us from then on 'to enjoy our own day-dreams without self-reproach or shame'.[20]

Might we not add, with reference to the distinction set up by Freud himself between the phantasy (or else the day-dream or waking dream) and creative writing, that the latter preserves a connection with the real, even as it is sharply detached from it – and primarily with the social – which relativises its 'egoism'? In this way, probably, it prolongs the play of childhood while adapting less well than it did to solitude. In every work, inscribed in it and discernible to others, there is the presence of some minimal social dimension, an appeal to witness which distinguishes it from any irrevocably insular phantasy.

So Freud's first written account concerning childhood is about play, phantasy and creative writing. The latter shares with phantasy a certain relation to childhood. But there are different kinds of works and, though he deals only briefly with this in his short lecture, Freud indicates two that are in contrast with the 'psychological' novel which he has principally in mind:

novels where the hero is more a spectator than a protagonist
and works whose material belongs to a collective and shared
repertoire of myths, legends and fairy tales. In some of Zola's
novels 'the person who is introduced as the hero plays only a
very small active part; he sees the actions and sufferings of other
people pass before him like a spectator'.[21] This type of novel
might appear further away than others from the day-dream or
waking dream, but Freud points out that he has encountered
variations of the day-dream 'in which the ego contents itself
with the role of spectator'.[22]

As for works which are not, strictly speaking, original
creations but 'the re-fashioning of ready-made and familiar
material ... derived from the popular treasure-house of myths,
legends and fairy tales', they pose a different problem which
Freud promptly resolves by shifting the analyses made at the
individual level onto the collective level: 'The study of constructions of folk psychology such as these is far from being
complete, but it is extremely probable that myths, for instance,
are distorted vestiges of the wishful phantasies of whole nations,
the *secular dreams* of youthful humanity.'[23] Ontogenesis plainly
replicates phylogenesis. In the schema outlined for this latter
type of work the dream is the origin of myth, which itself
inspires literary creation.

In other words, for Freud, dream (be it day-dream or night-
time dream) and literary creation share the same raw material:
childhood, which is defined as a mixture of memory and
repression, plotted by the psychoanalyst and expressed by the
creative writer. A year before his essay on 'writers and day-
dreaming', Freud had published 'Delusions and Dreams in
Jensen's *Gradiva*', a text in which he stated that the novelist and
the practitioner of the psychoanalytic method drew from the
same source and worked upon the same object:

Our procedure consists in the conscious observation of abnormal mental processes in other people so as to be able to elicit and announce their laws. The author no doubt proceeds differently. He directs his attention to the unconscious in his own mind, he listens to its possible developments and lends them artistic expression instead of suppressing them by conscious criticism.[24]

Thus the literary work and analysis can be said to proceed from the same object of which the dream is a part.

It is not the Freudian theory of literature that will detain us here. Indeed, we can take it for granted, along with J.-B. Pontalis, that Freud gives us a somewhat curt definition of literary creation when he set about looking for the primary cause and kernel of truth of all imaginative elaboration in the real facts of childhood.[25] My intention will be both more modest and more general. I should like to suggest that between dream, myth and literary creation, those three axes of the imagination, there operates a two-way circulation of images through which each one fertilises the others. From an anthropological standpoint, one might well surmise, moreover, that these images have more to do with death than with childhood and that their relation to childhood is also a relation to death. In those societies classically studied by ethnologists, early childhood was an ambiguous state, both because infant or perinatal mortality was significant (it has often been considered that a child was only truly born after several months of life) and because the newborn was identified in part with a being now dead of whom his body bore some trace or sign. More generally, childhood memories are associated with the face of beings no longer alive, the image of the child only returns with the procession of his witnesses: all those who once surrounded him, now distant phantoms or unrecognisable old men or women in the eyes of the adult who dreams or remembers.

The strange proximity everywhere affirmed between gods, ancestors and more recent dead must likewise be taken into consideration in any questioning of the nature of the imagined beings who people dreams and myths. In Africa and America a distinction has often been made between good and bad dreamers. The good dreamer is the one who can see clearly and who can identify the interlocutors whom he meets while he sleeps or, in the case of the shaman, during his long waking dream. It cannot be ruled out that the narrations of these good dreamers and the new actions of mythic heroes in the singular dream come to enrich the mythic source. In this sense, Freud's fine expression, 'the *secular dreams* of youthful humanity' could be made specific and contemporary: in its different forms, the singular dream is perhaps always one of the founts at which collective myth is nourished. This is what Michel Leiris suggested, as we saw, when he pointed out that the myth of the *zar* was enriched by the narration of earthly events whose genesis was attributed to them. This is what is stated by Georges Devereux in his *Ethnopsychanalyse complémentariste*, when, writing about the Mojave Indians, he says that myth is effective because it has already been dreamt of.

The way in which ethnologists 'collect' myths and their different 'versions' rarely corresponds to any pertinent sociological occurrence. The ethnologist is probably alone in attempting to collect an exhaustive mythic narration. On the other hand, we can see clearly, thanks to appropriate rituals, how fragments of myth and pieces of narration are used but also commented upon, developed and possibly enriched. This was the case at the sessions of divinatory therapy at which I was able to be present in the 1970s, in the Goun and Mina region, when the *bokono* was a recognised and prestigious personage. Mythical episodes which I knew from reading Maupoil, who had recorded them before the war (the *bokono*, however, could not read) reappeared in his mouth with sup-

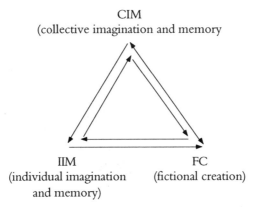

CIM
(collective imagination and memory

IIM
(individual imagination
and memory)

FC
(fictional creation)

plementary details and commentaries: the myth had undergone fresh developments. Perhaps one was even witnessing, at some potential level, the outline of a nascent epic, of a rhapsody composed by many hands. The mythical heroes of quite distinct pantheons are very standardised; they are characters more than people and, between one mythical episode and the next, one finds an identical and readily recognisable protagonist, including those episodes where the seer dealing with a specific case suggests a new variant. Thus the path of fiction, of the narration freed from all liturgies, may well pass through the dream and lead from the myth to the 'fictional creation' (literary creation, artistic creation) which re-stages its characters.

The collective imagination and memory (CIM) form a symbolic whole by reference to which the group defines itself and through which it reproduces itself at the imaginary level in the course of generations. The CIM quite clearly informs individual imagination and memories. Likewise it is a source for narrative elaborations (commentaries upon rituals, shamanic story-telling, epics) which are given form by creators with a certain degree of autonomy. The IIM (individual imagination and memory) complex can influence and enrich the collective complex, as we have just seen with Leiris, Devereux and the

Togo *bokono*, and it is a direct source of literary creation. Each
work of creation, whether it takes a sociological form which
is by and large collective, as in the cases of colonisation and
cultural re-creation, or a literary-artistic form which is by and
large individual, is liable in its turn to reverberate upon both
individual imaginations and the collective symbolic.

We shall posit the hypothesis that, as a consequence of this,
any drying up of one of these sources is liable to affect the other
two. This is the risk that we run today with the war of dreams.

ANTECEDENTS: THE COLONISED IMAGE AND THE COLONISED DREAM

History presents us with numerous examples of struggles over the control of images and the interpretation of dreams. There is nothing metaphorical about these struggles, even if there are times when they reflect internal conflict, as with the Church's attacks on the pagan imagination during the Middle Ages in Europe, and times when this is a conflict of a colonial nature, as in Mexico and the Andes during the sixteenth century, when first the mendicant orders, then the Jesuits engaged in what Serge Gruzinski has called 'the war of images'[1] against Amerindians who were not entirely unequipped in that department. A war therefore, a real war, right through the Middle Ages in Europe, as at the most blazing moments in the American baroque, a war of long duration whose complex scenarios demand the use of such terms as offensives, counter-offensives, strategy, confrontation, mobilisation, colonisation ...

In both the European and American spheres historians offer us extremely rich analyses. We shall have reason to dwell most specifically on three of the perspectives which they open up, since each of these highlights one of the corners of the triangle of the imagination which we have just sketched out. The first perspective, that of Jacques Le Goff[2] and Jean-Claude Schmitt,[3] lays out the relation between dream, story-telling and the formation of the self. The second perspective, that of Carlo

Ginzburg,[4] extends the first, one might say, pushes back its horizons, and places the experience of death at the source of all story-telling. The connections between dreaming and power are outlined in the third perspective, that of Serge Gruzinski, along with the different forms of confrontation between collective imaginations, giving scope for renewed inquiry into ideas such as syncretism, resistance or cultural re-creation.

DREAMS, VISIONS, STORIES

For the Church, the debate preliminary to any inquiry into the image has always involved the nature of dreams and visions. In the different contexts and at the different points in history where we see it confront the oneiric images of others, the Church swings between two attitudes, which, strictly speaking, can scarcely be reconciled: either images are nothing, mere vestiges of everyday life, corporeal residues, as if Christianity could only be materialist in the face of external cosmologies; or else they are illusions, false dreams which thereby, however, can be integrated variously into the Christian system of inter-pretation. The former position was adopted by the Mexican Church in a context where the true dreams/false dreams opposition was too tricky to work, given the traditionally very elaborated nature of how the Indians interpreted dreams. The Mexican Church, Serge Gruzinski notes,[5] took drastic action; it 'proclaimed in its preaching to the Indians that there was a complete split between sleep and the waking state, and it taught that the visual sensations which fill dreams or produce visions could be nothing other than reminiscences of impressions gathered in waking life',[6] even though, of course, one can never completely rule out the possibility of either God or the Devil intervening. Man, God or the Devil (the three sources of dreaming which are explored and analysed by Gregory the Great in the sixth century) are quite differently invoked and made use of according to the period and the circumstance. Historians are unanimous in stating that throughout the first millennium the Church's official attitude towards dreams was one of suspicion, even though it acknowledged in certain 'elite dreamers' (the expression is Jacques Le Goff's), essentially kings and saints, the capacity to have visionary dreams inspired by God. Apart from that, notes Jean-Claude Schmitt, average mortals were more likely to be regarded as an easy prey for 'diabolical illusions',[7] particularly while they slept. All through the High Middle Ages right up until the twelfth century, the distinction between 'true' dreams and false 'dreams' was connected to whether their origin was divine (guaranteeing the truth of the apparition or prophecy) or diabolical (the diabolical dream, which was just as real as the other kind, prompts deceitful illusions which dragged the Christian dreamer to his downfall).[8]

It is moreover normal that for an institution like the Church dreaming should be the object of extreme mistrust, given that by definition it eludes the control of the dreamers and *a fortiori* the control of those who are officially responsible for their souls, and given that ecclesiastics' own experience of it discloses the uncontrollable fevers and temptations that it can arouse, the abysses which it opens up in the imagination. Waking visions, which were apparently frequent, were held to be less disturbing both because they were produced before witnesses and because they were instantly subject to the appraisal and interpretation of the religious authorities. In contrast with the ungovernable night of the individual, which is exposed to the machinations of the Devil and the indulgences of the body, there is opposed the daylight of waking visions, which are filtered and secured by 'the testimony of authorised mediators who stand as a rampart against diabolical lures'.[9]

It is because men are mortal, and they know it, that dreams and visions are an opportunity for the Church to make everyone experience the uniqueness of a personal trajectory which after death is sanctioned by an individual judgement. Death plays an essential role here both because it is identified with the terrifying idea of that relentless judgement and because it is thereby the object of multiple testimonies which can assume the form of genuine narratives. Jacques Le Goff points out that the genre of oneiric autobiography saw the light of day during late antiquity and that the dominant theme of dreams recounted in this way is that of the journey into the beyond. On the basis of studying the 'autobiographical stories of revenants', Jean-Claude Schmitt shows more systematically the link which is progressively established between represen-tations of death and the dead, dream or vision, story-telling and the constitution of an autonomous subject. What we are to understand by the 'autobiographical stories of revenants' is the story told of an encounter with one of the dead (who may well be 'given the power of speech') by an individual, be it a monk or a cleric but equally, from the twelfth century on, an educated layman. The experiences which give rise to this encounter and the source of the story are of three kinds: the feeling of a nearby presence (a feeling akin to the 'disturbing strangeness', of the *Unheimlich* which Freud would be interested in), the waking vision of a dead person in a moment of ecstasy, and a sleeping dream. Historians are sensitive to the fact that stories told in the first person constitute one of the ways through which the individual has affirmed himself or herself. The development of these stories in fact takes place with the ending of the first millennium, following a widespread renewal of autobio-graphical writing and what we have come to describe as 'literary subjectivity'.[10]

Writing, private dreams and the work of mourning are therefore closely connected in an undertaking which Jean-

Claude Schmitt sees as all the more original for following on from a period (the first millennium) during which dreaming and the affirmation of an autonomous ego bore an equal weight of mistrust: 'the self conceived of itself and expressed itself through models of behaviour and a notion of identity whose points of reference were external to the individual subject'.[11] Thus it was the case that when Christians were asked to identify themselves, they simply stated their names as 'Christian', claiming no other identity than the one which they shared with their co-religionists.

Taken as a whole these commentaries are extremely interesting. First of all they invite us to consider that the idea of an autonomous self does not follow in the wake of Christianity like its shadow. The idea of community or communion is just as fundamental to it. What is needed therefore is a conjunction of elements, a conjuncture, for the accent to be placed on its singularising and individualising dimension. On the other hand, dreaming alone cannot constitute the essential experience of individuation. It does not offer to the sleeper's consciousness a series of discrete and precisely established identities. As for the sleeper's self, there are dreams or parts of the dream in which it plays no role.[12] For the story of the dream (or of the visions) to come close to a clear-cut manifestation of self-consciousness, something else is needed: a play of relationships through which is defined by its absence the place of a subject which it is the narration's precise task to fill.

One initial relation sets up the face-to-face encounter between the dreamer or the visionary and those who solicit his testimony – either private individuals or the religious institution itself, who formulate a request for narration and assist in the formation of a literary genre. From this point of view, the waking vision is distinct from the dream. The vision is first of all the object of an oral transmission, then a written transcription. Thus the story becomes a genuine 'social object', a quality which is also attached to 'the social space in which it is intended to circulate'. The autobiographical telling of the dream is distinguished from this first type of narration in so far as its signification and its margins 'remain frequently confined to the close circle of relatives and intimates who surround the dreamer as writer'.[13]

In this context, the dreamer or the visionary is a little like a traveller who is asked to relate his experiences. But we know where he has come from (he has travelled into the beyond) and who he has met (dead souls apparently anxious to maintain some contact with the world of the living). The experience of the dreamer-mediators of the Middle Ages is therefore not so distant from that of the Pumé shaman: their relationship with the dead dictates their literary inspiration and singularises their personality. The narrator's position is located at the junction of a social demand which is largely informed by the collective imagination and an imaginary experience which to some extent dictates individual memory and a personal relationship with death.

More than anyone else, the dreamer-narrator is thus in a condition to 'take his bearings' and gauge his position, between the living who wish to hear him speak of the dead and solicit his testimony and the dead to whom a special bond connects him, between the dead and his dead or, if we can put it this way (for everyone experiences the death of those close to them as projection and anticipation), between death and his own death.

Among historians of pre-modern Europe, it is probably Carlo Ginzburg who has given most thought to the question of the relationship between dream, myth and story-telling through their shared points of reference to death. But he approaches it on the basis of two distinct problematics which are quite separate, even though he attempts to reconcile them in his study, *Storia Notturna*. The first of these problematics is dictated by a hypothesis of a diffusionist type. A number of literary themes (the hero's journey in the Arthurian cycle as a journey into the world of the dead) and beliefs (the belief in werewolves in the Baltic countries at the end of the seventeenth century, and in the *benandanti* in Friuli between the seventeenth and eighteenth centuries) in his view derive from a cultural substratum which has Siberian shamanism as its archetype and origin. We should add that, for Ginzburg, this hypothesis does not obviate the need to inquire into the formal rules which enable the re-elaboration of the myth and the ritual transmitted through historical intermediaries. The whole problem, he adds (and this position strikes me as conveying an evolution of his theory, which was more firmly diffusionist to start with), is knowing whether, and to what extent, internal forms and rules 'are equally capable of generating isomorphic myths and rituals inside cultures which have no historical connections'.[14]

On a European scale, the similarity between the myths which converge in the theme of the witches' Sabbath is of particular interest to him, and behind this similarity the enduring persistence over millennia of what he calls a 'basic narrative kernel'. But the organisation of this narrative kernel no longer depends upon the random nature of historical transmission. It has to do with the second problematic, that of formal necessity in which metaphor (metaphorical displacement) plays an essential role, explaining the kinship between dream, myth and poetry. Hence the hypothesis formulated by the author, one whose boldness he himself seems frightened by. He writes: 'Perhaps the answer is extremely simple. Telling a story means speaking here and now with an authority which derives from having been (either literally or metaphorically) there and at that time. We have already recognised the participation in the world of the living and that of the dead, in the realm of the visible and that of the invisible, as a distinctive feature of the human species. What has been the object of analysis here is not one story among the many but the matrix of all possible stories.'[15]

To make the experience of death 'the matrix of all possible stories', is to take up a position which is firmly outside any culturalist or diffusionist problematic. It is to formulate the anthropological hypothesis of a necessary link between the imagination of death and all narrative imagination. It is therefore also to pose the problem of the relationship between myth, which is understood as a story of origins, and ritual, which is inspired by it but which reproduces and enriches it, fashioning the space where the dead return and where stories are wrought. If a link of this kind really does exist, it means that in situations of conquest and colonisation the stories and the dead from one side are pitted against the stories and the dead from the other. What Serge Gruzinski has called the 'war of images' stages this dual confrontation: corresponding to the statues and images of Christianity, launching its own ancestors on its conquest of the Indian imagination, are the exegeses and stories which recount its life and its miracles. If the experience of death is the matrix of all stories, then new images of death and the dead are the source of new stories. In fact, the cult of the Holy Death was to spread rapidly among the Indians and those of mixed race, and we well know how much the images of Christ's Passion were to influence them from the baroque period on.

Along with the historians of the extended European medieval period, we are able to see how the ambivalences and ambiguities of the Christian dream develop. Through the evolution of a phenomenon in which a series of binary oppositions (dream-revelation/dream-illusion, sleeping dream/waking dream, individual dream/collective dream) conveys the uncertainty which in some way forms it, one observation, nonetheless, progressively comes to light. It has to do with the importance always granted to oneiric images, to the close relationship they maintain with the status of the person and the individual, who is himself inseparable from the status accorded to the dead and to ancestors, and finally it has to do with their essentially narrative character, since, for external witnesses, but also for the one who has 'seen' them, they exist only through the story whose object they are.

The debates about the nature of dreaming, for their part, from the outset reveal its literally polemical character. Conflicts over dreaming are conflicts of interpretation and concern not just individuals. In *L'Imaginaire médiéval*, Jacques Le Goff points out that dreams interest historians as a collective phenomenon, that they are inscribed in the social and cultural contexts of a society and that the seventeenth century even saw 'epidemics of dreaming'. This collective aspect can become an expression of disaffection and thereby make those in authority uneasy. Even after the great wave of liberation for dreaming in the wake of the first millennium, the presence of the Devil, a presence behind which lay that of disaffection and heresy, was always suspected, especially when dreams seemed to be formed as a 'cultural counter-system' and the oneiric disaffection is linked to the heretical components. In relation to this Jacques Le Goff cites the case of the first 'popular' heretic after the first millennium, whose actions have their origin in a sleeping vision he experienced in a field, and that of the Cathars of Montaillou, who were so fascinated by dreams, as Emmanuel Le Roy Ladurie has shown. In the opposite direction, Jean-Claude Schmitt points out that in the period after the date of the millennium the stories of revenants, especially when they recounted a waking vision, were mobilised in the service of the reform of the Church.

THE WAR OF IMAGES

In the context of colonisation properly speaking, the clash of images would be even more shattering, though its consequences, to all appearances staggering, are all the harder to measure since added to the essential ambiguity of the phenomenon is the complexity of the reactions it entails, perennially divided between resistance and seduction. In different works, but most systematically in his book *La Guerre des images*, Serge Gruzinski clearly draws out the interplay of ambivalences which presides over the confrontation of imaginations in colonial Mexico. Indeed one outcome was that the Church worried about the success that was achieved, primarily thanks to the actions of the Jesuits, by the permanent and spectacular appeal to the Amerindian imagination, and which it strove to dominate or to redirect. On the other hand, the conversion of the Indians to Christian images is not unproblematic: we can quite equally observe their capacity to re-interpret these images, thereby privileging the hypothesis of an effective resistance and a sustained identity, or emphasise that in the long run the fervour of the Indians is the mark of an out and out adherence to the religion of the conquerors.

From this latter standpoint, we could give an account in military and triumphalist terms of the war of images unleashed by the Church in the sixteenth century. After the mendicant orders had prepared the ground by instilling some awareness of the canons of European art (likeness, perspective, the walls of images in Franciscan monasteries, the theatre and its make-believe), the offensive was unleashed around the middle of the century; the Jesuits were the shock troops; primarily, they outflanked the visionary experience of the Indians, replacing local pictography with the figures of European Christian art. The baroque battle plan, 'with its army of painters, sculptors, theologians and inquisitors',[16] would keep going until the eighteenth century, aiming to put the finishing touches to their integration of the Indians and the belief of an entire people, in a state sometimes close to hallucination, in the closeness of God and his saints. The issue will then be the entire society, Spaniards, Indians, blacks and those of mixed race, in an embryonic outline of national identity. The image clothes the body through tattooing and paintings: 'All distance is abolished between being and image on the white, brown or black skins of the inhabitants of New Spain.'[17]

But this one-way traffic (from one side's art to the other side's imagination) is oversimplified, even if it is plainly borne out, and, in the relationship to the image itself, what prevails is clearly ambivalence, whether among the Indian faithful, inside the Church or among those politically in charge. Let us take the example of the cult of the Virgin of Guadalupe, which remains a strong national symbol in the Mexico of today.

This cult goes back to the sixteenth century. Around 1530, a hermitage was built by the first evangelists on the site of a pre-Hispanic sanctuary, Tepeyac. The Indians visited the chapel most likely with a sense of thereby perpetuating the ancient worship of the Mother of the gods, Toci ('Our Mother'), a chthonic divinity. In 1555, probably under the initiative of Archbishop Montufar, a work produced by an indigenous painter, Marcos, after a European model but on a traditionally crafted support, was secretly substituted for the primitive image. Despite the protests of the Franciscans, the cult was to develop on this site which became that of the 'apparition ' of the Virgin. Is the term 'apparition' then applicable to the Virgin or to her image? Gruzinski points out that from an Indian perspective the question is immaterial: 'When we take a closer look, is it not the case that the apparition of 1555 is equivalent to the production of an *ixiptla,* in the ancient sense, in the sense in which the manifestation of a divine presence ensues from the making and presentation of the cult object?'[18] If it is to Archbishop Montufar that we must attribute the miracle's paternity, then he has won on all counts: he anchored the development of the Marian cult in a specific location, the ancient sanctuary of Toci-Tonantzin. He short-circuited the influence of the Franciscans, won over the Indians and bound together Indians and Spaniards in the same cult of worship.

In these terms, the politics of the image was announced by the Franciscans, who were more generally worried by the fact that a number of saints were being worshipped on the site of pre-Hispanic cults, and they suspected that many Indians were paying homage to their ancient divinities under cover of Christian devotion. The ambivalent positions of the Church, in all its diversity, would thus have a counterpart in the ambiguity, not to say the duplicity of Indian practices. Up until the end of the eighteenth century the cult of the Virgin of Guadalupe and the worship of saints in general would be regarded alternately by the Church with both enthusiasm and a certain amount of suspicion. Baroque piety reached its height in the first half of the eighteenth century, when local Virgins and miraculous images proliferated; then, faced with the onslaught of the Enlightenment and its rationalist thinking, the Church became more severe in its relation to popular devotion. The Society of Jesus, which had seen to the success of the baroque image, was expelled from New Spain in 1767. Now a distinction would be made between true miracles and false ones. It was important not to give the free-thinkers any opportunity to ridicule the true religion. The placing of greater value on internalised piety was accompanied by the decline of significant Mexican painting, the official abandonment of the baroque and a retreat from religious themes. But Gruzinski, analysing this planned disenchantment, stresses on the other hand the extraordinary vitality of the popular production of images which would still mark the whole of the nineteenth century. This output, which was sometimes the work of indigenous artists, 'tirelessly reproduced the souls in Purgatory, the lives of the saints, and miraculous Virgins, paramount among whom was Our Lady of Guadalupe'.[19] The monopoly of the image had shifted.

This ambivalence was also located at the political level. At the time of the War of Independence, it could be said that the two great Marian images were identified with one and the other side respectively: the Virgin of Guadalupe for the insurgents and the Virgin of Los Remedios for the loyalists: 'the Spaniards conceived such hatred for the Virgin of Tepeyac that they shot one of her effigies and desecrated several others'.[20] Following independence, Liberals and Conservatives alike turned Our Lady of Guadalupe into a national symbol. She was the patroness of the Mexican empire and would even seduce masonic circles. Though the official situation was modified after the fall of Maximilian's empire with the separation of Church and State and the constitutional reform of 1873, the cult of Our Lady of Guadalupe and devotion to saints in general were once again encouraged by the Church. And though liberals saw Mexican Catholicism as a form of idolatry, they could not ignore the great influence of the cult of the Virgin of Guadalupe. The Liberal Altamirano notes that her feast day was celebrated 'by Indians and thinking persons alike'.[21] Before her, social and ethnic origins were abolished and Liberal political thinking at the turn of the century, divided between rationalism and nationalism, could not but acknowledge her as an expression of national consciousness. It is on the whole quite remarkable that Liberal and lay equivocation over Our Lady of Guadalupe (seen simultaneously as a national symbol and a sign of obscurantism) should appear to echo the uncertainties of the Church, which was sometimes frightened by the excessive fervour and unalloyed devotion of its faithful to this image – as if it were compelled, more than four centuries after the Conquest, to continue having doubts about the real meaning of their conversion.

Doubts linked to the interpenetration and confrontation of different imaginations actually derive from different registers, even if one period or group should privilege one or other of them. The first of these is *representation:* one iconography fairly rapidly replaces another or superimposes itself upon the sites where cults are being replaced. This substitution–overlaying illustrates a relation of superior strength (the images no longer represent the same powers or the same entities) but quite quickly (in the space of a generation) it becomes the natural decor of daily life, the closest reference to the past which individuals of the second generation can remember. It becomes a second culture, in the sense that one speaks of a second nature, and even the only culture thereafter, as, over the generations, the power of stories and earlier references to the new collective history becomes dimmed. The second register is that of *the thing itself*, which can be too easily discarded by giving the name of idolatry only to the pre-Hispanic religions. What is really at issue in the debates which the Church orchestrates for its own purposes or to external purposes is the relation to the image and to the object, to the nature of their presence. Every image can prompt a phenomenon of appropriation and identification which confers upon it in return an autonomous existence of some kind and gives it a certain life of its own. This is true of the material image, even more so of the dream image and even more so still of either one when they merge, with the dream feeding upon everyday images and these in their turn seeming to be memories or extensions of the dream which has given them body. To turn all fetishistic devotion to Christian images into the unconscious trace of some lost idolatry or the indirect form of some tenacious resistance, is to argue like the Church, to enter into its rationale; it is, at any rate, to prohibit oneself from any deep inquiry into the nature of the relation that humans maintain with their imagination and their imaginary being. The third register is that of the *connective* or the *symbolic*. Once they have become material things, images are instruments of connection; in order to recognise them as effective powers or representatives of an effective power we have to be able to recognise ourselves in them (to recognise in them the identity that we share with others through them). Historically, the questions which affect the relation to the image simultaneously affect relationships between those who are its devotees. The heart of the matter, in the case of what is described as popular devotion, is the extent (this is a matter of interpretation and possibly a political matter) of the recognition effect which it provokes. When reduced to the single practising individual, this effect is unlikely to lead any further than an interpretation in terms of anodyne superstition. If it is projected onto the national level, it endows devotion, whatever one might bring to a scrutiny of it, with the value of integration. When reduced to a minority group, the recognition effect is readily felt by official authorities, be they religious or political, as potentially subversive. Underlying questions about the nature of devotion to images, about the truth of conversion or the paradoxes of obscurantism, there can be detected an anxiety which is more explicitly apparent on the occasion of some instance or other of popular feeling. For the identification aspect of the cult to highlight the individual or the national collectivity is, in the long run, eminently desirable. We have, besides, numerous examples of the politics pursued by the Church in this regard. But what is feared by the representatives of religious or political authority, without it always being formulated, is that the raising of the consciousness of identity which is born out of the practice of a particular cult should tend to demarcate the frontiers of the dominated group or groups, tentatively giving shape to forms of class consciousness and a will to resistance.

This fear and this doubt are significant. At heart they express the same uncertainty as the very movements about which they feel uneasy, which are never total either in their following or in their opposition. There is a rich literature about these movements, which are usually described as syncretic, that have arisen on every continent within contexts of colonisation. These contexts are themselves diverse but what they have in common is that they appeal to the imagination of both sides and that they modify their respective imaginary worlds. For all that, the contextual differences are not negligible. Thus the models of representation and interpretation in the Europe and America of the sixteenth century, at the time of the Conquest, were not so remote from one another as one might think.[22] But this 'contemporaneity' of coloniser and colonised has no equivalent in the nineteenth century during the European military penetration of Africa. We probably need to accord a special importance to the Enlightenment and to that modernity which was just as intent upon modifying those within its own close orbit as the distant lands to which the movement of European expansion had brought it. There are a number of examples which invite us to consider that the history of colonial America is a history in two periods: that of the Conquest (and of the relative 'contemporaneity' which we have just mentioned) and that of the formation of the state and the nation, in the course of which an elite of European origin emerges and reproduces itself by condemning the Indian, black or mixed race section of the population, which is democratically the majority, to a kind of political and ideological minority which for a long time will have religion as its only means of expression. The elite's membership of the religious models at issue may be sincere and spectacular on its part, thereby muddying the picture for any outside onlooker, but it 'differs', be it starkly or subtly, from popular devotion or composite movements, such as the Cuban Santería, the Brazilian Umbanda and the Venezuelan María Lionza, which were to proliferate on the outskirts of cities in the twentieth century.

BETWEEN TWO MYTHS

The suspicion of popular cults of devotion held by Christian elites is therefore that they are sometimes 'syncretic' (adoring one God through another God and, for example, a Mexican God through a Catholic saint), sometimes 'fetishistic' (confusing what is represented with what represents it), in other words either playing with the image or becoming distanced from it. This suspicion of difference is itself strangely ambivalent. It issues from an elite which condemns others to difference but does not therein acknowledge their right to wish to be different. As for those who see themselves thus paradoxically assigned to a difference which is simultaneously denied, they express something of this intermediary and contradictory status in their relation to the image. Specific devotion to this or that Virgin, this or that saint is not essentially different, in these terms, from participation in the deviant movements of the Catholic tradition which have two of their main theatres in South America and Africa. In every case, these cults have a history, but it is a relatively recent history. In the context of Catholicism it goes back to an apparition of the Virgin or to a special sign given by a saint, and the localisation of this apparition or this sign adds its weight of tangible reality to the shaping and picturing of the event. Outside the Catholic tradition, but often alongside it, it is usually a legend or the initiative of some personage or other which constitutes the founding episode. Through this return to the past the history of the cult resembles a myth of foundation, a myth of origin, but the origin can be recent and the foundation is unclear, insofar as the group whose existence it promotes has poorly defined boundaries, sociologically speaking. Each one of the cult's faithful maintains what is more like a personal relationship with it. On the other hand, the history of the cult does not constitute an eschatological myth. Its primary concern is the individual, but also the present. The image (the statue, the portrait, the object) is in some sense doubly present: it is there (and it may be a matter for discussion whether the Virgin is present in the image, or whether the image is itself her presence or whether it simply represents her) and it is there in the moment itself – in a perpetual present whose incessant reproduction is guaranteed by its presence.

The cult of the image is thus located at the heart of a history which could be defined as in a place 'between-two-myths'. As we know, the analysts of modernity have effectively identified two opposing types of myths: myths of origin, which locate the genesis of human groups and the cosmologies in which they have developed in a distant past, and myths of the future, eschatological myths corresponding to the modern time which makes the future the principle of meaning. In this perspective,[23] the passage to modernity corresponds simultaneously to an autonomisation of the individual, to the 'disenchantment' of the world (which itself entails a redefinition of the meaning attached to social relations[24]) and to the appearance of new myths, the myths of progress, the 'grand narratives' which will disappear in their turn, if we are to believe Lyotard, with the end of modernity and the era of the postmodern condition.

If we stay within the perspective of modernity (the one which prevailed as much throughout the wars of American independence and the subsequent efforts towards national construction as in the course of the nineteenth-century colonial episodes), the religious practices of the dominated or the colonised are clearly located in the place between-two-myths to which we have just referred: between a truncated past and

an obscure future. Of course, it is possible to give a more optimistic reading of the phenomenon. Thus Georges Balandier used the expression 'initiatives regained' to characterise the African religious movements ('prophesyism', 'messianism') in the wake of colonisation.[25] But if the regaining of initiative was indisputable, if certain forms of resistance or adaptation to the new situation were able to find in these movements some way of being expressed or being carried on, what is striking on the whole is more their historical incapacity to form real national Churches or to constitute any decisive political force. So the question is this: is not closure within a neo-cosmology of reaction the same kind of phenomenon as adherence to the religion of the conquerors or those who are dominant while being excluded by them? It is coupled with another question which extends and clarifies it: is it not the role attributed to the image in all these religious forms which cuts them off simultaneously from the past and from the future, locking them into the present and into what one could call new bubbles of immanence?

So what might be the common characteristics of this 'fixing on the image'? In the first place, for all its pretensions to re-foundation, it marks no radical break with the past. This is the sense of the Church's repeated interrogations about whether the faith of those whom it never stops regarding as neophytes is trustworthy. But it too has maintained this doubt through the procedures of substitution–overlaying, which compel it to sustain what is very like a form of double-talk regarding the image. This is also the meaning of the simultaneously vague and insistent references made by the so-called 'Afro-Brazilian' religions to an Indian or African past which is largely invented, and, more widely, by all the synthesising cults which proliferate in South America. It is furthermore the meaning of the double movement whereby the African prophets for their part attempt to mythify their own history (as indefatigable founders of a prophetic tradition which has heralded the coming of new times ever since the start of this century) while preserving fragments of cosmology and, more generally, diagnostic modes which attach them indisputably to a territory. These pasts glimpsed or redrawn with a somewhat quavering hand undoubtedly constitute a reference shared by many, but above all they support a mode of interpreting the real and the event in which relations between human beings always play a decisive role. This means that far from completely screening out the past which they make claims to conjure, such figures as the Christ of Sacromonte, the Virgins of Guadalupe and Los Remedios in Mexico, the Virgin of Copacabana in Bolivia, and their like across the whole continent (in a country such as Venezuela the twentieth-century has seen the appearance of a staggering number of very localised Virgins, the most famous of whom, the Virgin of Coromoto, established as the country's patroness in 1952, also found a place on the cult altars with strong links to María Lionza) set up or revive an enchanted relation to the world which is its most living expression, just like the *caboclos* of Umbanda or the African prophets.

The second feature common to these different cults is their individual character. This is not a question of individual salvation or of the psychological process of individuation. A religion of salvation such as Catholicism also has an everyday directional aspect, and the image stresses this aspect, if only because it is reproduced and multiplied. It is one of the characteristics of popular devotion that it transforms signs into presences; theoretically (from the standpoint of scholarly exegesis) holy pictures, medals and rosary beads only represent God and the saints, as *aide-mémoires*, possibly as calls to order, but we know very well that possessing and using these signs can give the devotee the feeling of presence and incorporation, as in the case of the tattoos and paintings which overload the 'baroque body'. In this sense, and in as much as one can claim to restore the subjective attitude of the practitioners, these signs-as-presences are not essentially any different from the objects which the pagan body takes on in order to protect itself from the hazards of existence and ambient ill will. Without departing from the merely descriptive level, it would be easy enough to show that the total number of sacred prostheses which are incorporated into the individual, in quite different contexts exercise a function which is simultaneously instrumental and connected to identity (in the same sense as in possession, where a reinforced personality can be born out of the disturbed liaison between possessor and possessed). This singularisation of the image or of the object which comforts and protects the individual encloses him in the continually threatened appearance of a perpetual present.

This situation in a place between-two-myths, or a mythic place-between, always gives precedence to the image, but it opens two pathways to the imagination. The prophet, the visionary or the rebel nourish their dreams with the image which mesmerises them and they seek fresh revelation through the dream. They dream about their childhood, hallucinate their present and try to imagine the future: the audience they may find in others encourages them to persevere and to construct a place where they can preach and which in their eyes assumes the value of a sign and of a presence. The prophets among whom I worked on the Ivory Coast were exemplary of this circular movement. In one respect or other they had all had dealings with representatives of Christianity, then, to set themselves up on their own, as it were, they had fashioned a personal myth, had reinvented their childhood, worked out a second-hand cosmology (on the basis of assorted borrowings from Christianity, from Islam even, and local cultural references) then at the end of all this, despite the universalist pretensions of their message, they had set themselves up in their native region. Their place of settlement (the 'new Jerusalem',

as some of them called it) then became at one and the same
time an abode, a hospital, a place of shelter, a temple and the
centre of a territory to which there applied what one might
call a private cosmology: a spatial and mental enclosure which
simultaneously marks out the end of a road followed and the
contradiction of a step taken. The abode of the prophet,
whatever the story played out, enacted or repeated there, is first
and foremost his imaginary world come true, or, to be more
accurate, an imaginary coming true.

The second pathway opened up to the imagination in this
situation of a place between–two–myths is that of art. The two
paths can, moreover, mutually interfere with each other. With
some of the African prophets one cannot avoid being aware
of the originality of the *mise-en-scène*, the magnificence of the
costumes or the beauty of the singing. In South or Central
America I have noticed more than once the efforts made by
the somewhat marginal personalities of local cults, whether
close or not so close to Christianity, to fashion some pictorial,
plastic or literary work. These autodidacts of religion, art and
literature did not always have a very easy nor a very balanced
personal life, as if they had been caught unawares in the currents
and counter-currents which complicate navigation from one
axis of the imagination to the other. But, in the case of Mexico
(and, more broadly, of Central America), artistic creativity was
the Indians' natural response to the flood of images which
swamped them, and, as we have seen, this creative urge survived
the Church's changes of strategy. The Indian art which imprints
its own hallmark on works inspired by the Christian tradition
is perhaps a good thing for the art of Ibero-America, but this
success does not however bring any immediate solution to a
situation of closure of which it is instead an expression.

It has to be pointed out that, be it for the inventors of the
sacred or the creators of images, the situation of the place
between–two–myths is one that condemns to repetition and

replication. Either of these can be carried out with greater or lesser degrees of talent, greater or lesser degrees even of personality, but they are above all the products – the reflection and the echo – of a fascination which none of the works ensuing from it can possibly dissipate. Once the new religion or the new vision of the world has brutally replaced the old cosmology, inside the triangle of the imagination the mesmerised reproduction privileges a one-way relation between the new collective stereotypes and the individual imagination; this is so with the African prophet whose cosmology is only a pale reflection of those which inspire it while casting nothing back; or between these same stereotypes and the axis of fiction-creativity; it is so with Indian artists all of whose talent is sapped in the reproduction of the image produced by others without creating any new genre. One could even suggest that the aesthetic struggle waged during the baroque period reverses the movement which leads from the dream to the work. The strategy of conversion can also be understood as a strategy of inversion and appropriation with the intention to shape the imaginary world of the Indian dream according to the imaginary world of an external art – a process of exhaustion which, one might fear, would completely dry up the living fount of creativity. Elements induced from outside into American or African cosmologies, whether at a religious or artistic level, provoke the appearance of a mesmerised consciousness which experiences the greatest of difficulties in re-creating a universe of original meaning. At least these difficulties allow us to glimpse the place in which strategies of re-composition and re-creation can be worked out in the long term: in the colonial and postcolonial context, creativity, both plastic and literary, blends images from Christianity with other images and other references; thus there is a possibility of new individual syntheses as, for example, borne out by the boom

in South American painting and the novel. But the path is a
narrow one and may be cut off from here on.

Nowadays, there are detours and short-circuits that spring
to mind. Where Mexico is concerned, Gruzinski points out the
parallel which could be established, regarding images, between
the sixteenth and the twentieth centuries. Mexican muralism
(one of the great pictorial experiments of the early part of the
century, as exemplified by painters such as Orozco and Rivera)
strikes him as a 'distant reverberation, in a secular version, of
the Franciscan image' aiming to celebrate the heroes of
Independence and the Revolution. Nowadays, and with even
more unquestionable success, 'the legendary rise of Mexican
commercial television under the aegis of the Televisa company
has all the appearance of the miraculous, all-embracing imagery
of the baroque period returning in full force'.[26]

Put in these terms, the connection between the baroque past
and the 'postmodern' present – a prefigurative connection –
could be regarded with relative optimism. The American
experience of mixed ethnicities and languages, of cross-bred
imaginary sensibilities, of conjoined memories from Europe,
Africa and America, has this at its heart, if we return to the
closing statement of *La Guerre des images*, 'how better to face
the postmodern world by which we are devoured?'[27] Without
taking issue with this observation, nor ignoring the specific and
exemplary character of the American experience of the image,
we can suggest two complementary ways of throwing light on
it. We can consider first of all that the situation of the mythic
place-between is characteristic of all colonial situations, that it
blocks, as it were by definition, all access to any effective
modernity – as defined according to accreted criteria of the
autonomy of the individual, of disenchantment with the social
bond and of inscription within a historical progress which has
democracy as a stage and a condition. But we must admit, on
the other hand, that in certain respects it prefigures a situation

which is now widespread across the whole planet. This made me wonder about African prophets in the early part of the century and whether they had not been particularly aware of the acceleration of history, the shrinking of space and the individualisation of human destinies whereby one could alternately define the colonial situation and the contemporary situation of global 'hyper-modernity'. The whole problem is then one of knowing what is represented sociologically and historically by this short circuit, this impasse in the way of modernity. We can also ask ourselves questions about the present of the most technologically advanced societies, about their relation to the image, about the contemporary forms of confusion between reality and fiction, and we might wonder whether we have not entered (we, that is, humanity) a new phase of a mythic place-between which obscures our perspectives on the future. The question can be formulated differently: what is now our imaginary universe and are we still capable of imagination? Are we not witnessing a generalisation of the phenomenon of mesmerised consciousness which we have viewed as a feature of the colonial situation and its different avatars?

THE THEATRE OF OPERATIONS: FROM THE IMAGINARY TO THE 'ALL-FICTIONAL'

THE TRIANGLE OF THE IMAGINATION: SUBSTITUTION-OVERLAYING

When we looked at notions of selfhood brought into play in the phenomena which are seen by ethnologists as archetypally dream and possession, there seemed to be two of these: the aggregative notion and the alternative notion. Even if these two notions do not so much constitute an opposition as the two extremes of a configurative spectrum, their existence and their role in the construction of the relation of self to self and of self to others, which defines any individual trajectory, underlines the importance of the connection between 'individual imagination and memory' (IIM) and 'collective imagination and memory' (CIM), two of the corners of our triangle of the imagination. The works of historians, for their part, highlight the connection between the experience of death (in which the first two imaginations intervened) and fiction, in the guise of the subjective literary narrative. Freud, who attributes the source of the work of pure fiction to the individual's imagination and memory, gives a separate designation to a number of literary genres (myths, legends and fairy tales) in the construction of which collective imagination and memory (what he calls the *secular dreams* of youthful humanity') manifestly play an overriding role. Moreover, we have been sensitive to the fact that the IIM axis, which is essential in the birth of literary fiction, equally plays a part in the enrichment and development of the CIM axis, through the channel of dream interpretations or commentaries on ritual sequences.

In an attempt to appreciate better the imaginary dimension of phenomena of contact and cultural conquest, we shall provisionally make an abstract schema of the reflexive effects linked to individual initiatives. Thus we shall try to pinpoint the phenomenon of overlaying which we mentioned in the previous chapter, and, more broadly, the situation of the mythic place-between. In the original situation (pre-Hispanic, for example) and, once more, independently of the reflexive effects of the IIM axis towards the CIM axis and the fiction (CF) axis, the central role is assigned to the CIM axis which informs both the individual imagination and works of art or literature.

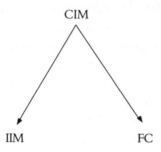

The contact situation is sensed first of all as the arrival of new fictions — of new stories and new images. There is always an interval, however brief, between the first contact or the passage to the act of conquest and the unleashing of the ideological project. The tools of the new message at first constitute a new fiction which will exercise its own seductive powers over the CIM and the IIM.

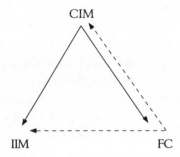

Of course, it is not enough for the project of colonisation to have the status of a 'curiosity'. It is more a case of this being how it itself designates the imagination of others, unless it turns it into the dark side of its own truth (the proof that the Devil exists). Its stories and its images must occupy the place of the earlier CIM, re-model the IIM and recreate the new art. A shift in the opposite direction assigns to the earlier CIM the place of fiction (in this case folklore). The result then is a schema which is strictly homologous to the previous one were it not for the fact that the aforementioned fiction becomes the new CIM which in turn informs the IIM and FC axes; but the FC itself takes in the old CIM which, once the permutation is complete, now only exerts its influence upon the CIM and IIM as fiction.

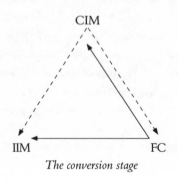

The conversion stage

We are referring here only to two extreme situations. The permutation is never total nor is it completely in evidence: the anxieties of the Church, its internal disagreements over strategies of the image bear this out well enough. But it is certainly one of the crucial issues which we see clearly emerging within the phenomenon of colonising the imagination; a putative trial of strength, where guile sometimes exerts strong-arm tactics to gain mastery of the other's images. It is interesting that in not one instance is there, strictly speaking, any total blotting out or exact overlaying, since the imagination of one group can only constitute a collective imagination for the other group by the exporting of their own imagination into fiction. The superimposition, therefore, goes hand in hand with a time-lag which complicates its reading and interpretation.

The same thing applies whenever the 'grand narratives' of modernity appear. Modern discourse is bent on occupying the place of the collective memory, on re-building memory on the basis of a founding event (the French Revolution, for example) in order to open up the imagination to the future. In the case of the South American countries, this event is national independence, whose image carries the association of heroic figures (Bolívar, General San Martín). This new foundation sometimes entails a re-casting of what has preceded it. The Spanish conquest is no longer celebrated as such but, on the contrary, in terms of the phenomena of resistance to which it gave rise on the part of the Indians. Thus it was that, in the cult of the hero, which for some time would be one of the official expressions of Venezuela's nationalist ideology in the twentieth century, the figures of the Indian *caciques*, the symbols of a resistance greatly re-imagined by artists and intellectuals, would join those of Bolívar, his black comrade (Negro Primero) and the leader of the slave revolt against the Spanish (Negro Miguel).[1] Miscegenation is the official state doctrine and the intellectual tool of a national affirmation.

Of course, here, too, the permutation is not total. The secular state comes to terms with the Church. The latter means to play its part in the building of the nation, and the cult of the hero, even in its popular variants (like the cult of María Lionza) are no real substitute for Catholicism, and even less so for earlier references which it can, on the contrary, revitalise. We also know the difficulties which revolutionary France, and later the USSR, encountered in effectively symbolising their secular or atheist ideologies. The fact is that, in the name of progress, the ideal of modernity tends to relegate the entire corpus of religious affiliations to the axis of fiction by a movement analogous to the one which ordained the confrontation between religions.

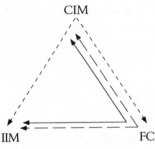

The disenchantment stage

However, only a simultaneous scrutiny of the different figures can allow us to grasp the precise sociological situation, one which combines two situations of the mythic place-between which are themselves unstable: in the first place-between a tension is expressed which is linked to the project of conversion, and in the second it is the tension between the modern imagination and religious imaginations. The enchantment of the world, moreover, notably in the form of the enchantment of the social bond which constitutes its perennial form, is one of the stakes in the religious struggle which has no place in the modern imagination. We know that ideas of the miraculous, of exorcism and cures through prayer are themes alternately effaced and re-activated by the Christian tradition as a part of its strategies of conversion.

The question is obviously one of knowing the nature of the connection between the three axes of the imagination, even now that just about everywhere the death is being announced of the myths of modernity – which in their turn would become mere elements of fiction. But taking on this question presupposes a double reflection: on the image, the material image to which human beings now are even more exposed and sensitive than in the baroque period, and which changed its character from the moment when it became a moving image; on fiction itself, which one might speculate has also changed its nature or its status from the moment when it seemed no longer to form a specific genre, but to espouse reality to the point of merging with it.

THE SCREEN PHASE

The author to whom we must refer at this point is Christian Metz,[2] because he has considered both the image and fiction in the cinema from a psychoanalytic perspective. We shall look at the perspectives which he has opened up in three directions: the status of the character, the process of identification and the comparison between the 'filmic state' and the 'oneiric state'.

There has been a classically established distinction between the fiction of the theatre, which rests essentially on the actor, and the cinema, which directs the spectator's attention more towards the character, prioritising the 'representer' in the one case and the 'represented' in the other. This difference, drawn out by cinematic theory, had likewise been observed, notably

by Octave Mannoni,[3] for whom, Metz tells us, 'even when
the spectator identifies more with the actor than with the role
(rather like at the theatre), this identification is with the actor
as "star", as yet another character, someone fictional and fabled:
in his very best role'.[4] The interesting point here alludes to the
existence of two levels of filmic fiction, which can, moreover,
be combined without any immediate contradiction. Jean Gabin
is Jean Gabin (with his own history, his legend, his love affairs,
and, even more, his silhouette, his cocky humour and his
personal tics) but he is also the seasoned gangster whose story
we follow with interest, as if each one of the two fictions fed
the other. We know that, especially in the category of films
known as B movies, the actors can end up always playing the
same character, who then becomes confused with the actor,
at least the actor in the second sense maintained by Mannoni,
the star who is herself or himself a character. The two characters
only add up to one. Actors towards the end of their careers
(Gabin, John Wayne) could be reproached with no longer
acting anything but *their* character. But this kind of identification has its charm, its virtue in the effective sense of the term.
We often find the plots of films summarised as if the actors were
effectively the protagonists ('Then Gabin tells Delon: take the
dough'). Thus is set up the system within which we can be led
to believe that we know these people because we recognise
the characters.

This confusion makes the cinema akin to myth: mythic
episodes, however different they are, always present us with
characters who are identical to themselves, and easily caricatured
– the gods of Olympia have had no trouble turning into comic
characters. The same comparison with myth also exists in
television series; it would be even more accurate to say that
these have a mythic dimension. The success of the big American
series (whether these take the form of serials – though in this

case each episode nonetheless has its own coherence and relative autonomy – or a sequence of separate little stories, in the setting of a police station, a law practice or a cruise liner, an unchanging decor which reinforces the recognition effect) derives from the expected, surprise-free character of their different heroes. We are glad to re-encounter those we have the feeling we have always known, glad therefore to recognise them. In this respect, cinema moves even further away from the theatre the closer it gets to myth and television series. The charm of classical theatre, for example, derives from an effect which is strictly the opposite of what defines popular cinema, television series and myth by homology. A fresh interpretation brings with it a rediscovered character. Tartuffe, the Miser and the Misanthrope are as different as the actors who embody them; Jouvet's Tartuffe was nothing like Ledoux's: we don't recognise them though we thought we knew them. A play cannot live for long except through the 'revivals' which it receives over time.

Christian Metz believes that he can generalise the distinction and, obviously thinking of the great roles personified for ever in the eyes of cinephiles by the names of certain legendary actors, he specifies, thinking of Mannoni's two levels of fiction: 'If the film role is forever tied to its interpreter, it means that it is his performance which catches the actor's reflection and not the actor himself, it means that the reflection (the signifier) is recorded, and can therefore never vary.'[5] It is interesting to observe how these days the American film industry with increasing frequency makes attacks on the link which, in accord with Metz and Mannoni's view, one could argue as a necessary one between the film role and its performer. Don't these attacks jeopardise the theatre/cinema distinction or do they have other implications?

First the facts. It is plain that American producers buy European films not with the intention of distributing them in transatlantic cinemas but in order to film them all over again. They buy them rather as one buys a patent, for the right of reproduction. These films (for example in recent years, the French comedies *Trois hommes et un couffin* and *La Cage aux folles*) are then filmed with American actors[6] in an American setting. The script is not at issue: it is usually re-done word for word, down to virtually the last line of dialogue. The reason invoked in support of this switch to an all-American get-up is 'what the public wants', which is therefore to imagine the public as being allergic to any over-obvious local colour. To be quite clear it comes down to something quite different from mere local colour. Local colour can find its place in Disneyworld, in exotic restaurants or in 'Cultural Studies' departments – precisely as local colour, with everything this term suggests of the stereotyped and limited, indeed of the potentially fictional. As creative works, films are not pure fictions: they are, one might say, a claim to everyday evidence, to existence; they suggest a space, a history, a language, a way of looking at the world, with the specific they aspire to the universal. And one is inclined to suppose that it is not European actors as such who lie behind the references to 'what the public wants' but what Christian Metz calls their 'reflection', as if Americans ought not to be allowed to think that other mythologies, other histories, other ways of looking than their own might exist, as if, beyond the multiplicity of cultures-fictions, there could be only one true collective imagination.

The best proof of this is that once these films have been re-shot for the American audience, they are re-exported, primarily to those countries that sold the script for them in the first place. How much more naively, or more imperially could it be asserted that what the American audience 'wants' prefigures what any possible audience could – which is certainly by now partly the case, so much have ' mass audiences' worldwide become used to the landscapes, rhythms, speech and expressions which translate and construct, with extraordinary effectiveness besides, a global and all-encompassing vision – a vision, which is to say both a way of seeing and the reality which is its object.

The re-shooting of foreign films is not the same thing as the re-make. As something closer to the theatrical 'revival', the re-make has been around for a long time. More often than not it falls within the same cultural history as the original and it may go through a re-writing of the script. Nevertheless we can consider it too as deriving in part from a hijacking of mythology. It can besides be combined with an Americanisation of the references; it was in the United States that a new version of *Les Diaboliques* recently came out. As in some Amerindian mythologies or in some popular cults, new figures arrive to replace those which, being thus obliterated, enter legend a little later, soon to exist only in the memory of the very old or of experts, and rising to the most prestigious but the most distant regions of the world of gods and ancestors. Harrison Ford appears; Bogart and Brando are already far off. The re-make is a remedy for nostalgia. It re-founds myths, it slides mythology a bit further on. It is in tune with the acceleration of contemporary history whose setting in motion of the image was after all its sign and its evidence, since the impression of movement depended upon the technical capacity to accumulate the greatest possible number of still images in a single second.

Filmed images therefore confront us from the outset with a dual paradox: the illusion which they disseminate is of a piece with the reality which they record; and we rediscover ourselves in them even though they are the product of another's way of seeing.

What does it mean that we rediscover ourselves in them? It means, first of all, that the spectator 'believes' in the story which unfolds on the screen. Of course, he or she knows that this is a fiction and does not really believe in the reality of what is in front of their eyes. But the fact that they cannot 'believe' in the story in this sense is corrected by the fact that they could, that they were able to believe in it once, that they could still believe in it if they were children, the children they perhaps are still. With adults, 'the beliefs of earlier times irrigate the disbelief of today, but they irrigate it by denial (one could also say: by delegation, by shedding the belief onto the child and onto former times)'.[7] What the sociologist Isambert has done is remind us, in the case of Santa Claus, of the 'proxy' belief handed on to children by their parents which permits the latter to enjoy this past belief through them.

Is it then something from childhood that we rediscover at the cinema? There are a number of indications inviting us to answer this question in the affirmative. To begin with, at the cinema, we are small. We have to look up (as in prayer to this or that religious effigy) to see those who fill the screen. The big screen, so well-named, is in the first place a device which returns us to the proportions of childhood, the time when landscapes were so vast and when adults were physically matched with their status as 'grown-ups'.

Childhood rediscovered, then, but, at one and the same time, childhood to be built and to be left behind: in the second part of his book, primarily in the sub-section titled 'Note on two kinds of voyeurism', Christian Metz investigates the comparison which has been made possible between the relationship to the screen and the mirror phase. This comparison strikes him as risky. What the child sees in the mirror is in fact the image of his or her own body. In cinema as we know it, the image of the spectator does not feature on the screen. There is therefore no process of identification, as in the mirror, around a subject–object (this self which is another) but around a pure subject, a subject who is 'all-seeing and invisible, a vanishing point in monocular perspective taken up from painting by the cinema'.[8]

At this point two themes intersect: that of the *seeing authority* and that of the spectator's *sub-motivity*. The body of the cinema spectator is motionless, even if some spectators move around more than others, and we'll return to that. The state of sub-motivity, in any case, refers to the spectators' state of passivity, 'absorbing everything through their eyes, nothing through the body'. This passivity facilitates identification both with the camera eye and with the projector or, to be more precise, with the entire process of screening which constitutes the film. What matters is not so much identification with the characters in the film, something already secondary, but what precedes it, the preliminary identification 'with the seeing (invisible) authority which is the film itself as discourse, as an authority which sets out the story and offers it to be seen'.[9] The question of sub-motivity itself brings us to an examination of the relationship between the film, more specifically the perception of the film, and states like dreaming and hallucination.

The combination of sub-motivity and heightened perception was already associated with the mirror phase by Lacan. Christian Metz, who refuses to compare the relation to the screen with the mirror phase, embarked upon a more systematic examination of the relations between what he calls the 'filmic state' and the 'oneiric state'. In order to do this he begins with a number of empirical observations. There are times when the audience participates in the action of the film with speech and gesture. The force and the frequency of these motor irruptions depends either on the nature of the audience or on the nature of the spectacle (thus the crowd's participation becomes an integral part of the spectator sport). As distinct from these very specific occurrences, which are also very rare among European cinema-goers, we must cite states of 'mental unbalance' during which the spectator has the feeling of waking up, as if for a brief moment he or she had seen a piece of the film as a dream. Christian Metz defines this moment as 'a step in the direction of the true illusion'.[10] Lastly, it is common knowledge that when someone has not had enough sleep, there is a greater risk of drowsiness during the screening than before or after it. The sub-motivity can thus be the cause of a 'paradoxical hallucination'.[11]

The hallucination is paradoxical in the sense that the subject hallucinates what was really there. Its existence is connected to the state of the motionless and mute spectator who pushes the 'perceptive transfer' further than the spectator who is restless and interventionist, because the former invests in perception the energy with which the latter fuels his activity. It is therefore genuinely a matter of a hallucination 'from the tendency to confuse distinct levels of reality and from a slight temporary fluctuation in the testing out of reality as a function of the Self'; but it is a paradoxical hallucination 'because it lacks that quality characteristic of the true hallucination, of fully endogenous psychic production'.[12] It is in their 'gaps' that the filmic state and the oneiric state can be compared; there are times when one believes that one has dreamt or hallucinated what one has really seen, but there are also times, during dreams, when one knows one is dreaming.

Christian Metz takes from Freud his ideas of the 'progressive way' and the 'regressive way'. They are useful to him in establishing that the degree of vigilance and the degree of illusion of reality are in inverse proportion. In the waking situation the pathway of psychic excitations starts out from the external world, passing through the perception/awareness system to end up in memory traces localised in the pre-conscious or the unconscious. The regressive way, conversely, starts out as in the sleeping dream, from the pre-conscious or unconscious system, to end up in a perceptual illusion which can go as far as hallucinatory psychosis. The mediation and evocation of memories take the regressive way but not right to the end. The filmic state too fulfils certain conditions of the oneiric state. Even if the logic of the reality principle (arising from the realism of the images and perhaps also from the spectator's surroundings) is more pronounced in the film than in the dream (which obeys processes such as displacement and condensation), the film is 'riddled with emergent primary material'. Christian Metz is able to conclude that going to the cinema means 'lowering the ego's auto-defences by a notch'.[13]

This lowering of ego defences corresponds to the particular relation which film maintains with 'fiction', defined not as the capacity to invent fictions but as 'the historically constituted and much more widespread existence of a regime of socially regulated psychic functioning, which is accurately called fiction'.[14] Fiction is a fact before it is an art or before certain art forms take it over. We can only therefore ask ourselves about the way in which individuals 'rediscover' themselves in a fiction, in a film for example, if we take account of the regime of fiction to which it corresponds.

If fiction can indeed be defined as a socially regulated regime of perception, it follows on the one hand that it has a historical existence which is expressed in institutions, methods and practices, and on the other that it amounts to a socio-cultural fact which plays a part in relations of alterity, and interconnections of different kinds. Christian Metz takes up these two points with regard to the cinema. Hand in hand with the cinema as an art are professions, technologies, an industry, a market, etc. What matters, from the standpoint of the audience's relation to the film, is that the development of this industry acts retrospectively upon the psychic effect which made it initially possible and profitable. We can therefore assume that the 'regime of fiction' can evolve simultaneously with the genres and the works whose genesis it has made possible. From their first appearance, the techniques which are specific to the cinema brought about an upheaval in the regime of fiction:

the specific nature of the cinematographic signifier, with its peculiarly 'life-like' photographic images, with the real presence of sound and movement, etc., has the effect of inflecting the albeit very ancient phenomenon of fiction towards historically more recent and socially specific forms.[15]

One is hard put to see how the accelerated development of technologies of the image could not have had a huge influence on our own regime of fiction, ever since the cinema's golden age, and particularly with the emergence of television.

But let us stay for the moment with the cinema as an example, in order to examine the second point in question: fiction as a socio-cultural fact playing a part in relations of alterity. If the pleasure taken in the spectacle of the film comes through a lowering of the ego's auto-defences, through a narcissistic withdrawal and a self-indulgence in phantasy, a supplementary paradox of filmic perception nonetheless makes it possible to define it as an unusual experience of opening up to others – unusual in two senses: because it is rare and because it is of an extraordinary intensity. By an effect which is simultaneously distinct from identification with the 'seeing authority', the film as a mechanism, and from any secondary identification with the characters, the perceiving subject then *recognises* the existence of an Other (the author) analogous to himself or herself, analogous to the I which is the subject of the perception. Perhaps one could suggest that, in these rare moments, the 'screen phase' reverses the effect specific to the mirror phase: the Other is an I.

Undoubtedly any work, if it bears the stamp of an author at all, can at any point produce an effect of recognition or of affinity. But in the case of a non-visual work this effect is transmitted through the mental images produced by the person reading it or listening to it. It is this work's capacity to appeal to his imagination which he values in the first place, not, strictly speaking, the coincidence of his own images and those – which, by their very nature, elude him – that the author might well have 'had in mind' when he or she was fashioning the work. One could even say that in this case the unusual quality of the imagination freed by the work gives a measure of the affinity that it can arouse. It is a common experience, by contrast, that a visual work, for instance a film, can strike us as inferior to the dreams whose memory we retain and to the reveries which we manufacture for ourselves. This is because we are then brought face-to-face with images produced by an other.

If phantasies are the fulfilment of wishes, in these terms they will always be superior to the images produced by others, which are after all merely the realisation of other phantasies. Freud, as we have seen, was surprised enough by the miracle of literature, which, to a greater or lesser degree, made it possible to identify with someone else's phantasy. But when the work itself is an image, the phantasies of the author and those of the spectator are in headlong collision, and Christian Metz, in agreement with Freud that other people's phantasies 'repel us or at least leave us cold', appropriately points out that, whenever he goes to the cinema, 'the reader of the novel does not always find *his own* film in it, for what he is looking at in the real film is now someone else's phantasy'.[16]

This analysis has its place in a very specific regime of fiction. In the case of the statues, holy pictures and staged performances to which we have referred, the 'works' are located at variable distances, depending on the period and the individuals, from the axis of the collective imagination and from the axis of fiction. The author is often conjured away; the statue of Our Lady of Guadalupe just ' appeared' out of the blue in the guise of the Virgin herself, and it is likely that in the eyes of many the latter is undifferentiated from the former, like the represented from its representative. The connection to the image is therefore direct and personal; it can be literally 'incorporated'. It is likewise 'symbolic', in the sense that it sets up a link between all those who recognise themselves in the same image. This, besides, is laden with official and well-known exegeses; the personal phantasies which converge on the image − but without being recognised as such − adapt all the better to this shared dimension and this common rhetoric for their acting as supports in the real world.

It is altogether different in the relation to the work which is recognised as fictional. Of course the fact that a work is a work of fiction as much in the eyes of its author as in those of the public does not thereby define it as alien to or counter to the real, not just because the latter is its raw material, in a variety of respects, but because there can arise collective, social, if not religious phenomena around the work and in relation to it − for example, there are cult films which rely on the complicity of cinephiles.

But the basic primary dimension of the work of fiction is transmitted by way of the author's potential relationship with his or her audience (a book is written to be read, a film made to be seen) and by way of the audience's reciprocal relationship with the author, this being an actual relationship because it obviously assumes the completion and reception of the work. In every case this relationship is imaginary and that is what makes it interesting: it produces contact between singular imaginations. Admittedly, in the case of the film, this relationship to the author is the less obvious, as we have seen, because it imposes its images on the spectator, and it is usually enough for the cinematic illusion to produce identification with the mechanism of the film and with the characters. Let us say that the 'screen phase' is not an obligatory stage for reaching cinematic pleasure. In fact the fit between filmic images and the phantasies of the spectator is never guaranteed. But:

when as a matter of chance it is granted in sufficient measure, satisfaction – the sense of a small miracle, as in a shared state of amorous passion – is due to a certain effect, one infrequent by its nature, that can be defined as the temporary breaking of a very normal solitude. It is the particular joy which lies in receiving from outside images which are usually internal, images which are familiar or not too dissimilar, and seeing them set down across a physical space (the screen), and thus discovering in them something almost attainable which was quite unexpected, and feeling for a moment that they are perhaps not inseparable from the mood which most often trails after them, that sense of the impossible, so common and accepted, which is for all that a form of mild despair.[17]

There is something Proustian here in the mention of a 'small miracle'. Only, if the fortuitous episode which awakens the corporeal memory of Proust's narrator brings him the proof of his own existence, what is given to Metz's spectator, thanks to a coincidence of images, is rather the proof of the Other's existence, or an other at any rate; this is simultaneously a tangible proof of reality and a minimal proof of sociability – the end of the phantasy as solitude and of solitude as destiny.

Fiction can therefore be the opportunity for the individual's imagination and memory to experience the existence of other imaginations and other imaginary worlds. But this experience rests simultaneously upon the existence of a fiction which is recognised as such (of a way of looking at the real which does not merge with it and which does not merge either with the collective imaginations which interpret it) and upon the existence of an author who is recognised as such, with his or her unique characteristics, and who thereby sets up a potential bond of socialisation with those who constitute his or her audience.

STORY-TELLING AND FREEDOM

The status of fiction and the place of the author are therefore in the end the two criteria whereby a regime of fiction can be defined. This is not to say that every work of fiction is 'signed' (singularised and individualised) as a film or a novel can be in the modern Western tradition, but that some gap, a feature of the work itself, is always signified between the fiction and the reality which matches it, just as between the person who has conceived of it and those which it is about. The art of signifying this gap is perhaps the key to the *ars poetica* and the condition of 'preliminary pleasure' of which Freud speaks. But it is not tied to a specific genre. Let us for example consider the *Légende de la mort*. This is a collection of tales translated and edited by Anatole Le Braz,[18] who collected them in Britanny from different story-tellers, or more simply from different interlocutors ('informants', ethnologists would say). The lived quality and relative anonymity of these tales is modified by two specific effects. The story is often presented as a story within a story – bringing to mind the picaresque novel. This procedure sets up the distance between the teller and what is told, and *a fortiori* between what is told and those who listen to it. These stories, these 'lived' adventures, which in certain respects recall the autobiographies which medieval historians talk about, were told during vigils, but often a vigil is a starting point for the plot – another distancing device, by analogy as it were, or, as Freud would say, a 'playful' one: the story plays with its ambient reality, gets close to it, slips away from it for a moment and moves off. The teller plays with his listeners, who play at being frightened. The teller is certainly in the position of an author (it is of no importance whether he is or isn't the inventor of the tale: he is identifiable and he identifies fiction) and each one of the listeners, in this precise and culturally defined moment (this is a vigil), is free to let his or her imagination wander. The 'enchanted' connection to the world is not exclusive of the pleasure to be had from making it an object of narration (either as teller or listener) and, by the same token, standing back from it, albeit only a little, while between the teller and the listeners themselves a bond of complicity arises which is yet another testimony to the 'fictional'[19] quality of the story. From this standpoint, irrespective of its content, all identifiable fictionalising is a priming of 'free-thought' in relation to the representations of the collective imagination. And, if we go along with Ginzburg when he sees in the experience of death the matrix of all story-telling, we can further add that all story-telling is at the same time the initial act whereby men free themselves from the obsession with death. In this sense fiction which is recognised as such is fundamentally liberating, but the freedom which it brings about remains in tension with the respective imperatives of the two impulses of the imagination which simultaneously stimulate and limit it.

Writing about 'Forms of Belief and Rationality in Greece',[20] Jean-Pierre Vernant tackles the question of the connection between belief and fiction. After having investigated the rituals and depiction of the gods, he notes that in Greece the object of belief is what is told through the narration of myths. For a long time orally transmitted, some of them have been fixed as written versions: 'in Homer, Hesiod and everything we call the epic tradition'. These texts, these stories are distinguished by an enormous diversity and thus there are many more stories than there are in Hesiod's *Theogony* to narrate the genesis of the gods. In this open and undogmatic 'religion', belief was 'of the kind which one accords to a story that one knows is only a story'. In other words, the tale told by the Greek poet, the inspired bard, is at the same time the development of a collective memory, the expression of a knowledge 'which constitutes the social cement of the group' and ... a story. The two axes highlighted in this way, the axis of belief and the axis of fiction (of the clear awareness of the partly imaginary and fictive nature of the tale) are never totally separate. The question arises whether the gap thus designated by Vernant between belief and fiction is not, more broadly, a component of affiliation, through literary pleasure, to the polytheistic religious models or the polytheistic aspects of monotheistic religions. In any case I am struck by what appears to be a gap of the same kind in the attention given by the Pumé Indians to the stories of the shaman who evokes their gods and their dead or in what Anatole Le Braz records of the old Breton vigils. In every case, an aesthetic distancing (the measure of freedom simultaneously acknowledged for the author or the story-teller and for those who read or listen to them) brings about a slight discrepancy (a 'play' in more than one sense of the word) between the constraints of the symbolic system and the imagination of the individual. This experience of literary 'play' is perhaps the obligatory preliminary to any development of philosophical thought and the intellectual freedom which it institutes in relation to established cosmologies – a freedom which moreover assumes the existence of writing as a guarantee of memory and a support for argument.

FROM THE NARRATIVE TO THE 'ALL-FICTIONAL'

It could be that this experience of freedom under constraint is now being called into question by the new regime of fiction. In it the status of fiction and the place of the author are effectively overturned: fiction invades everything and the author varnishes. The world is penetrated by a fiction without any author. Everything which encourages the development of a new kind of orality is in danger of appearing in the long run as the instrument of philosophical regression and critical thought in retreat.

Let us go back briefly to the diagram with which we tried to outline the effects of overlaying specific to the periods of conversion and disenchantment. First we saw the stories of Christianity taking over the axis of the collective imagination which had previously been occupied by the pagan imagination, with the latter slipping away towards the axis of fiction. In the phase of disenchantment, we saw the appearance, first as fiction, of the grand narratives of modernity which progressively replaced Christianity, relegating it to the axis of fiction, in order in turn to occupy the axis of the collective imagination. We have now reached the point where the grand narratives of modernity are also being snatched away by the axis of fiction. But there is nothing to replace them on the CIM axis and they have ended up in the fiction position in the same manner as the previous collective imaginations. We have arrived at the 'all-fictional' – in the same sense as we use the term 'all-electric'.

All the old collective imaginaries now have the status of fiction. But once the axis of the collective imagination is unoccupied, there is no place for the relationship between the individual imagination and the CIM axis, a two-way

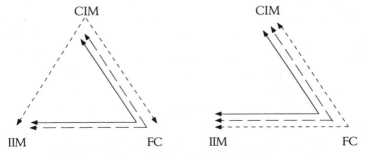

The transition to the 'all-fictional'

relationship which we had provisionally plotted into the diagram. The individual imagination no longer faces anything but fiction. But fiction too has changed since it no longer connects by exchange with the CIM axis, now unoccupied. The diagram becomes simpler. The new fiction, which we shall call fiction-image, is situated halfway between the old CIM and FC axes – as if each of them had slid towards a new balancing point. The CIM axis, which is directly linked to this new balancing point, has no connection with anything else now. Informed by the fiction-image alone, the self which occupies the former axis of individual imagination and memory (IIM) can be said to be 'fictional'.

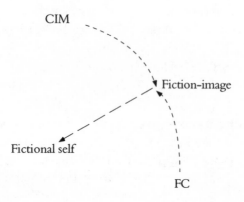

The fictional self is unceasingly threatened by being absorbed by the fiction-image which stands in for both the collective imagination and for fiction, while owing its existence to their elimination, to the simultaneous disappearance of history and of the author.

It is probably necessary at this juncture to indicate again that each of the diagrams sketched out here represents an extreme case. The overlaying of conditions of the imagination, in an empirical situation, assumes the co-existence of old diagrams and more recent ones, each with its specific effects of overlaying and discrepancy. So it is in no way true, for instance, that history has ended and that there are no more authors. It is in point of fact the dominant ideology which decrees the end of history and assimilates created works as products like any others, because, like any ideology, it privileges and generalises one aspect of the real. But it is true that, taken to its extreme, the logic of the hyper-modern situation assumes or postulates this double disappearance. It probably also needs to be made clear that it is not our intention here to offer an evolutionary theory of the imagination where each exemplary instance would follow on from the one before like the turn of the seasons, even if we have managed to give the reader this impression about each of them. They are, rather, new possibilities which history gives rise to. They co-exist, even if each of them is respectively the expression of certain forms of power and is, on a global scale, fought over as a crucial issue. The imagination has its own efficacy, we well know, but, from the standpoint of battles in history, there can be a question whether it is not more a means than an end, or, more accurately, whether it is ever confused with the ends with which it is associated. The ideology of modernity has gone astray on this point by allotting inevitably interdependent destinies to the forms of economy, society and imagination.

The question is more one of knowing whether the development of technologies has released, essentially as the work of those who use them for economic and political ends, a misdirected form of the imagination ('fictionalising') and with it a harmful energy of which they no longer have complete control and whose existence, in truth, they have not fully recognised. The disaster would be for us to realise too late that the real has become fiction, that there is therefore no more fiction (only what is distinguishable from the real is fictive) and even less so any author. We have got to the point of 'fictional' explosion just as with nuclear catastrophe: it may not be fatal but it has become possible. The most serious thing is that, in the case of a 'fictional' explosion or implosion, there would be very few survivors. Like David Vincent, they would strive in vain to wake up the unconscious and beatific victims, the 'fictional' selves, to call them back to their lost imagination and lost memory.

So there is some point in listing the first signs of the disaster and locating the future theatre of operations. The image first of all, the televised image. We are compelled to recognise that there are great differences between the 'filmic state' and the 'televisual state'. At first sight, we could even think that the ego defences are less threatened by the latter than by the former. The television mechanism is different from the film mechanism. The spectator's gaze does not identify with it as the 'seeing authority', as at the cinema. Everyday decor remains in place (a flat, a cafe) and the light is usually left on; people can still chat among themselves. The screen is small, at eye level — at least for now. For all these reasons, when films or telefilms go out on the 'small screen', identification with the characters is less immediate. On the surface, the possibility of changing channels, of 'channel-hopping', gives the TV viewer a power of selection and decision which has no equivalent for the film-viewer at the cinema.

But everything that distinguishes television from the cinema at the same time opens up other, more insidious opportunities for identification and hallucination. In the first place television is quotidian and familiar. For many people it is the organising principle of their time, day in, day out, week in, week out, year in, year out. Like the early Catholic bells, it punctuates the hours of the day. Like any liturgy, it announces the week's prayers and services. Like any religion, its forms follow the seasonal rhythms of the year. With this it brings into every household faces which are all the more familiar for being expected at fixed times, and because they are felt to have been chosen – if need be by changing channels at any point. Thus the home becomes filled with household gods, small domestic divinities who are pleasant, and dependably even-tempered. The male or female figures who enliven the game shows, present the weather forecast or comment on the day's news over time become as indispensable to the household as those who really live there. Firm likings, sometimes dislikes, are formed for them. They are rarely the object of indifference. They are stars without being actors, as if the small screen instantly guaranteed those who regularly appear on it the status of a fictional character analogous to that of the actors who have won it by dint of a brave struggle under the studio lights.

In the second place, it is fiction's status itself which is less guaranteed on television than in the cinema, for on it the gap between what is fiction and what is real becomes less discernible. This is already so with the everyday 'stars' to whom we have just referred. Some of them offer us the most concrete aspects of the reality which surrounds us (the weather, small news items, political events, sports results) but it is as 'stars', as already fictional characters, that they enter into our everyday private lives. The choice of a news programme is often dictated by the image of the presenter on that channel. This slight vagueness in the distinction between what is real and what is fiction extends to other aspects of televisual perception. Let us quote a few at random: the heroes of American television series have such a presence on the screen that in their case the character absorbs everything to do with the actor. Of course, Peter Falk can be interviewed, but in everyone's eyes he is and always will be Colombo. Of course, some actors manage to move on to another role and sometimes even from the small screen to the big one. But the indissoluble link between the character and the actor remains the key element of television series. This indissolubility, which endows them with a mythic

aspect, has as its corollary the extreme realism of the sets and
situations. The police stations, law practices and courtrooms
of the American series are carbon copies of reality. The fictions
they stage look like reportage. I remember arriving in New
York one day, turning on the television in my hotel room, and
thinking for a few minutes that I was watching a series I had
seen some episodes of before, where a skilful lawyer strutted
his stuff convincing juries and taking apart the prosecution's
case, until the point when I realised I was looking at a live
broadcast of Judge Thomas in the courtroom. This was,
moreover, a trial which was so popular with my New York
friends and colleagues that, for all their conscientiousness and
niceness, they would get home every night as early as possible
so as not to miss the next act of the soap opera.

We should mention in the third place all the cases of 'fictionalisation', of turning the real into fiction, in which television
has been an essential tool from the moment when television
stopped imitating real-life and real-life began reproducing
fiction. This 'turning into fiction' is connected in the first
place to the overabundance of images and the consequent
abstraction of how they are viewed. The televised image levels
out events without being able to deploy layout and different
kinds of typography as in print publications. Whatever the order
in which events are presented and regardless of the inflections
in the presenter's voice, the images follow on with no break:
thousands of dead in a flood somewhere far away, a *coup d'état*
in Africa, a football league replay, a motorway accident. We
are called on as witnesses, caught between some doubtful
innocence (that of the bombardier who drops his bombs from
high in the sky) and a faint sense of guilt, of a debt in relation
to the victims of catastrophe or epidemics who urge us to make
our little contributions to the telethon or some other charitable
set-up, perhaps to ward off the threat of misfortune. For us as
obviously passive onlookers, the pile-up of disasters is combined

with the variety of landscapes which are simultaneously remote and close: a global play of reflections dependent on the whim of the remote control button.

From time to time, all references to any reality whatsoever disappear. Thus advertising plays upon the supposed effects of its prior repetitions and proceeds by way of allusion, by self-referential quotation: the opening bars of a tune, the outline of a well-known image reminds us of whole sequences and, by extension, of the excellence of a brand of coffee or a car. Television itself willingly become its own object and narrates the glorious hours of its brief history as if it were ours too, and indeed it is inasmuch as we have lived through and by the image.

The effect of levelling out works not only on situations but also on people and characters: in the televised Olympus, side by side with the leading lights of politics, entertainment and sport, we find likewise the puppets who imitate them, the characters who resemble them and the journalists who present them – all of them stars and 'fictional characters' in the sense used by Christian Metz, and compelled moreover to exist as fictional characters in order to exist as political, artistic, even scientific personalities. What matters is not what these personalities think about their entry into fiction so much as the effect produced by this fictional levelling on those whose access to the world outside is mainly through television.

The effects of levelling out can be ascribed in large part to the images themselves, now that the mass media are condemned to multiply them, to produce and reproduce images without interruption. But the image is no longer the only issue once real events deliberately use it and, as it were, define themselves through it. During the Gulf War and, later, during the landings in Somalia, we were virtually summoned in front of our television sets in order to witness the start of operations, live, at the appointed time. The fluctuation in the distinction between what is real and what is fiction here becomes clearly ascribable to a genuine staged production. In these particular instances, the show did not entirely live up to the publicity and the expectation, but it reinforced the fictional dimension of the event: in the eyes of the spectators, alleged witnesses to a war of which they saw nothing, the Gulf War looked like a video game about warfare, demonstrating the precise and 'surgical' nature of the Western operation. Here we should bear in mind the need for the politico-military event to exist as a spectacle and the obligation placed on citizens to be witnesses to a fictional event.

Until now we have gone no further than the image perceived, and the forms in which the image is received. In a way, we are still not very far from the position of the cinema spectator. We are merely observing, and this is a lot in itself, that the frontier between the real and fiction becomes less distinct and that the author, even if he or she does exist, is absent from the television viewer's awareness. But there are other signs which indicate that the 'fictionalisation' of the world is under way and that it is taking place not just through the image.

Strangely enough, for one thing, not content with looking at images, human beings in general (but males in particular, as if the camera were as necessary to them as the steering wheel of their car), amateurs and tourists set about producing them. Not so much to create a work, to make art (even if amateurism – 'people's art' – can be decked out in technical and aesthetic references and dressed up in the somewhat old-fashioned elegance of an elitist terminology now popularised or, as is said of certain sports, 'democratised')[21], as to accumulate evidence of their having been in places which they scarcely had time to see. 'The world is designed to end up as a good book', wrote Mallarmé. 'The world is designed to end up as a video', is the answer given with one voice by the tourists of every nation who travel the world, it is true (the world near or far, according to their means and the rate of exchange), but they travel with one eye riveted to the camera, as if this journey in future perfect could have meaning only once it was over, during evenings spent in the company of relatives or friends resigned to playing the part of witnesses as they watch the film of a peregrination which has finally ended.

This, then, is the completion of the movement at whose end the truth of what the subject has experienced (or has not experienced) and of the subject himself (since he too can feature on the transparency or in the film with the help either of certain devices or an obliging bystander) is transferred to the image and on to the screen which supports it. If we go back now to that expression 'the screen phase', it is therefore no longer a question of recalling the effect of abrupt affinity which turns an other into the equivalent of an I – in the miraculous moment described by Christian Metz – but of a time-lagged face-to-face encounter whereby the subject identifies with a past image of himself or herself. I is another, perhaps, but this other is no longer there.

With each day that goes by, the world itself is increasingly organised to be visited, but even more so to be filmed and, ultimately, projected on to a screen. Every night the world's high spots light up, but more and more we are offered the spectacle of what we ourselves go there looking for: images. Anyone who climbs Mont Saint-Michel to reach the 'marvel' of lace set in 'stone', undergoes not just the assault of the money lenders and traders in the Temple (they existed long before provoking Christ's censure) but that of the traders in images whose wares show off the Mount in staged poses: filmed from every angle, caressed by aerial cameras, plunged in darkness to be lit up, rising from the waves in a re-found glory. The voices of well-known artists, no less, narrate its legend. Stereo recordings of the most famous orchestras send a shiver down the unclothed spines of summer visitors. After this, what is left to see and, worse still, to film? They have come too late to a world seen too much. Yet, tenaciously, they do film; if need be, they film the film, with flash bulbs going off in the darkened cinema. As if, in this final reflex, they were offering the proof that they still exist. Doubtless knowing their customers through and through, those in charge of some of the travel agencies envisage taking them on advance trips to sites of interest in three dimensions on the Internet. This touristic *hors d'oeuvre* will not in the end be any more virtual than tourism in the future perfect from behind the camera. And the tourist of the future will most likely not be discouraged but stimulated by the technical perfection of the trailer offered in this way, since he will always have to travel to the site he likes best to bring back images of his 'own' making.

Encouraged by its early successes, the project of fictionalisation becomes as a result more ambitious: it creates new worlds in the middle of nowhere: theme parks. Disneyland is the archetype: a fake American village street, a fake saloon, a fake Mississippi, Disney characters who roam around all these fake places, a fake castle with a Sleeping Beauty, go to make up the decor of a fiction raised to the third power. Fiction (primarily that of the European fairy tales) was brought to the screen, then back down on earth for the sake of receiving visits – an image of an image of an image. And what will the visitors do? Set about filming, of course, put back in their black boxes all the characters who should never have left them, while making the most of the opportunity of seeing them in person – or having them seen, at the very least, in the presence of their nearest and dearest: wives, children and grandparents who can all get together soon to watch themselves on the screen (on the TV screen, what's more) along with Mickey, Donald and Prince Charming.

Theme parks, holiday clubs, leisure parks and residential ones like Center Parcs, but also the private towns which are seeing the light of day in America, and even the fortified and security-patrolled residences which are springing up in the cities of the Third World, like so many fortresses, form what one might call bubbles of immanence. There are other bubbles of immanence to be found, for example the big hotel chains or stores which reproduce more or less the same decor, can the same kind of muzak in every department or in their lifts and offer the same easily identifiable products from one end of the earth to the other. Bubbles of immanence are the fictional equivalent of cosmologies: they are made up of a series of indicators (plastic, architectural, musical, textual) which make them recognisable, and they draw and mark out a frontier beyond which they are completely unaccountable. They are both more material and more legible than cosmologies, which are symbolised visions of the world; their apprenticeship is easier; but they obviously lack a symbolic, a prescribed way of relating to others (which in their case is reduced to a code of good conduct among users) and a system for interpreting events (even if they set about fabricating miniature worlds, microcosms of the macrocosm wherein is proclaimed the dignity of the consumer who visits them). They remain parentheses to be opened and closed at discretion, with the use of finance and knowledge of a few basic codes.

Nowadays, it is the circle, the repetition and the echo which are the dominant figures on an enormous variety of scales. Satellites go round the earth to observe or photograph it. Fixed in place, they function to bounce the images transmitted from one side of the globe down on to the other. The chain stores, as the name suggests, clasp the earth. Decor recalls decor, advertising advertising, the copy wants to be a copy, everything becomes recognisable, everything turns back to where it started.

Fiction, from this point on, becomes even bolder; not content with creating new parentheses, it attacks the real itself in order to subvert it and transform it. This is a relatively minor matter when it makes do with putting out background music in a supermarket or in the tunnels of the Barcelona Metro (thereby occasionally giving the person walking through them the impression of striding across a screen somewhere towards the happy ending of a Technicolor movie), but it becomes more ambitious when it undertakes to re-model the forms of the city according to its own criteria. A few months ago, there was a press announcement that the Arquitectonica studio as designers, along with the Disney Corporation as promoters, had been the winners of a competition organised by the City Hall and the state of New York to build a hotel and a commercial and leisure centre on Times Square, and for the restoration of the nearly hundred-year-old New Amsterdam hotel on Forty-Second Street in Manhattan. Similarly, the Disney Corporation seemed to have been given the job of developing an entertainment programme in Central Park and of building a department store at 711 Fifth Avenue, where all the merchandising lines from its films could be bought. One is struck by the spectacular nature of the project: the new hotel will have 47 floors and 680 rooms; it will be designed with a gap where a 'galactic ray' will pass through'; as for the Disney Vacation Club, it will take shape as a sort of gigantic container holding 100 apartments and covered with ten huge television screens, one for every floor, and a host of neon signs. But the most extraordinary thing about this project is that right in the middle of the city, like a normal part of it, it sets up the world of Superman, itself initially conceived as an imitation of the city, a fiction in a fictive city. The two winning architects have opted for an aesthetic of chaos, but it is very deliberately the chaos of comics strips and cartoons. As some journalists [22] have remarked, the project under way in Times Square is faithful to the aesthetic of enter-tainment centres already in existence in the United States, an aesthetic which keeps well away from any debate about the meaning of the work. The Disney effect takes itself seriously and is self-referential, forming its own point of reference for the future. Fiction imitates fiction.

If we take Disney as an example – it is, all in all, just the most successful concern in the business of fictionalising or spectacularising the world which is so characteristic of our time – it gives us an idea of what a world of pure fiction would be like. But to a large extent we are already in such a world. And the 'non-places' which I happened to mention elsewhere can be judged above all in terms of their fictional capacity, their capacity to fictionalise. One is never very far from Disneyland in an airport or a big hotel, and it is moreover very seldom that one does not come across some traces of its presence there on a poster or in a window display. Mickey's ears are listening all over the world.

To judge the extent of the fictionalisation phenomenon, there is one observable starting point: if the fiction is a good fit with the technology (to the point that it becomes one of its dominant themes in amusement or leisure parks), it is because the technology itself fits very well with the fiction, and with all fictions. Hyper-modernity, as we live it, proceeds from an improvement in technology which is itself only a spin-off from science; the environment which it creates has the appearance of a second nature and in itself bans no ideological option. We can even assume, given the relative isolation entailed by connection to the image nowadays, that the technological environment should prove propitious to solitary varieties of escapism, such as consulting a horoscope, listening to music with a headset or trying to link up on an Internet site with interlocutors who are voiceless and faceless but, like oneself, possessing the power of speech. In the United States a great diversity of religious leaders (Catholics, Anglicans, Muslims, Jews, Mormons and even Zen Buddhists) have set up web sites on the Internet.[23] They have found the first results to be encouraging, especially for the great religions, Catholicism in particular. Thus more than 300,000 people linked up with the Vatican web site in the two days following its opening (at Christmas 1995). The editor of the Holy See's Net pages told the *Financial Times* that it was easier for people to use their computer than to go to the library and read encyclicals. The Islam web site has already attracted 7000 people. But the best demonstration of the compatibility between the Internet and religion was supplied by the reception given to an initiative by the Hebrew Centre for Communication in New York which put on to the Internet a detailed document about the history and customs of the Jewish people that has 200,000 users a month. Those running it do not rule out the possibility of turning the site into a thoroughgoing commercial undertaking which would rent out space for classified advertisements. But according to the director of the Centre, Larry Yudelson (and this is what most strikes our attention) what encourages the Churches to conquer this new platform is above all the private nature of the relationship which is established between the user and the Net. Religious experience, some conclude, might undergo an upheaval as a result, with Masses able to be celebrated and confessions heard on the Internet. One can also imagine that, faced with these countless opportunities for 'à la carte' religion, some would be tempted to practise their own brand of continuous mystical DIY, re-creating for their exclusive use spaces for some mythic place–between analogous to those we think we have pin-pointed in situations of a colonial type. To each, for a while, his own cosmology.

The question to be asked in the end is whether all the connections which are set up through the different media, whatever their likely originality, are not from the outset a matter of a symbolic deficit, a problem in creating any social bond *in situ*. The fictional self, the peak of a fascination which is begun in any relationship exclusive to the image, is a self without relationship and as a result without any basis for identity, liable to be absorbed by the world of images in which it believes it can rediscover and recognise itself. For a while I happened to work with a lively and likeable young man of around 30 who every morning gave me a running commentary on the news. I had no trouble following his commentary, having already heard it (as he had, of course), word for word, on a private radio station a few minutes earlier. This man was nonetheless in perfectly good faith and he identified with what he was saying. I sometimes caught myself imagining that one day he would tell me his latest dream and I would recognise it as mine because we would both have seen it on television.

THE AGENDA

I gave this book the sub-title 'Exercises in Ethno-Fiction' because I had two expressions in mind and two attendant concerns. The 'ethno-sciences' always set themselves two goals. As a prefix, 'ethno-' relativises the term which follows it and makes it depend upon 'ethnicity' or 'culture, which are assumed to have analogous practices to those that we call 'sciences': medicine, botany, zoology ... From this standpoint, ethno-science attempts to reconstitute what serves as science for others, their practices of looking after themselves and their bodies, their botanical knowledge, but also their forms of clas-sification, of making connections, etc. Of course, once it becomes generalised, ethno-science alters its standpoint: it tries to put forward an appraisal of local, indigenous models, and possibly to compare them to others and, furthermore, to suggest an analysis of cognitive procedures in operation within a given number of systems. It then sometimes goes by the name of anthropology: thus one talks about medical or cognitive anthropology.

Ethno-fiction might be defined in accordance with these two standpoints: on the one hand, an attempt to analyse the status of fiction or the conditions of its emergence in a society or at a specific historical point; on the other hand, an attempt to analyse the different fictional genres, their connection with the forms of the individual or collective imagination, with representations of death, etc., in different societies and at different conjunctures.

I am aware of having done no more than sketch out this twofold course. The fact is that it was just as important to me to produce a work of ethno-fiction, in the same way as we talk about science fiction, whatever its failings. Because the truth is that the war of dreams has begun (and that we must attempt to imagine its future developments and its possible consequences) and what is also true is that we cannot always clearly see the ins and outs of it right now. This uncertainty about our precise situation should not prevent us from acting, from striving to define an ethic of action, rather like Sigismund, Calderón's hero in *Life is a Dream*, who, impelled by a cruel experience early in life, decides to all intents and purposes to behave as if he were dreaming and would one day wake up.

If the 'fictionalisation' of the present is now replacing (or adding to) the mythification of history, the first enchantment (the mythification of origins) and the second (the mythification of the future), if it is in its logic to produce an equally 'fictional' self which is incapable of setting its reality and its identity within an effective relation to others, we must define not only an ethic of watchfulness, 'in case of awakening', as Calderón's hero does, but an ethic of resistance.

This would rest upon some simple acknowledgements. In the first place models should not be confused with reality. Likewise we can heap up lots of very concrete examples of the enchantment of the world, even in the most technologised sectors of the most 'advanced' societies, likewise we should know that ideas about disenchantment, about the end of grand narratives, about hyper- or postmodernity, about 'fictionalisation', refer to models which are partial views of a real that authorises them but does not merge with any one of them. In the second place, the image is an image. Whatever its power, it has only the qualities with which one endows it. It can seduce without alienating, however much an entire system might strive to turn it into a tool of stupefaction. The fate of the image does not belong to it. Nor does ours.

Who will be tomorrow's resisters? All of those who, renouncing neither past history nor history to come, will denounce the ideology of the present in which the image can be a powerful point of relay. All of those creators who, somehow or other preserving the circulation between the individual imagination, the collective imagination and fiction, will not give up incurring the miracle of the encounter. All the dreamers, finally, who are skilful enough to cultivate their own phantasies so that the off-the-shelf imagination of the illusionists of the all-fictional becomes an object of private derision.

All those in short who are more concerned to construct modernity than to short-circuit it.

Without this kind of vigilance, there is a risk that a portion of humanity might be caught in the proffered game of mirrors so that it would seek itself therein unendingly and unendingly become lost. Liberal totalitarianism has no need of Big Brother or of Tabir Sarrail – Ismael Kadare's Palace of Dreams. Let us remember what Sartre said about the dream defined as fiction, but fiction that 'bewitches', about the dream of a consciousness which has made up its mind to transform everything it takes hold of into imagination, just as 'King Midas turned everything he touched into gold':

> The dream is not fiction taken for reality, it is the odyssey of a consciousness committed by itself, and in spite of itself, to give form only to an unreal world. The dream is a privileged experience which can help us to conceive what a consciousness would be like which had lost its 'being-in-the-world' and which, as a result, would be deprived of the category of the real.[1]

Let us be vigilant.

NOTES

THE NUB OF THE SITUATION

1 Paul Hazard, *La Crise de la conscience européenne, 1680–1715,* Paris, Fayard, 1961: 'When Leibnitz saw that Europeans could not be stopped from fighting, he suggested that they direct their fierce bellicosity outwards ...' (p. 409).
2 *Le Monde,* 9 March 1994.
3 Georges Charachidze had developed his position at greater length in his article 'Les Tchetchenes, un peuple en sursis', *Le Genre humain* 29, 1995.
4 In Jean-Michel Sallmann (ed.) *Visions indiennes, visions baroques: les métissages de l'inconscient,* Paris, PUF, 1992.
5 S.F. Sundkler, *Bantu Prophets in South Africa,* London, Oxford University Press, 1961 (first edition 1948).
6 *Non-Places: Introduction to an Anthropology of Super-Modernity,* trans. John Howe, London, Blackwell/Verso, 1995.
7 Georges Devereux, *Ethnopsychanalyse complémentariste,* Paris, Flammarion, 1972.

WHAT IS AT STAKE: DREAM, MYTH, FICTION

1 B.G.M. Nadel, *Nupe Religion,* London, Routledge and Kegan Paul, 1954.

2 Jean Pouillon, 'Malade et médecin: le même et/ou l'autre', in *Fétiche sans fétichisme*, Paris, Maspero, 1975.

3 Luc de Heusch, *Pourquoi l'épouser? et d'autres essais*, Paris, Gallimard, 1971.

4 There are of course examples of dreams 'of general interest' (politics, in particular). Caroline Humphrey gives some examples from Mongolia, where it is possible 'to dream for someone else, and even to dream for a number of other people': Caroline Humphrey and A. Hurelbaatar, 'Rêver pour soi et pour les autres', *Terrain* 26, 1996.

5 A good account of different forms of 'dream' analysed in the literature connected with the idea of personality is to be found in Giordana Charuty, 'Destins anthropologiques du rêve', *Terrain* 26, 1996.

6 Gemma Orobitg, *Les Pumé et leurs rêves*, Paris, Éditions des Archives Contemporaines, 1998.

7 Jean-Pierre Dozon, *La Cause des prophètes: politique et religion en Afrique contemporaine*, followed by *La Leçon des prophètes*, by Marc Augé, Paris, Éditions du Seuil, 1995.

8 Michel Leiris, *La Possession et ses aspects théâtraux chez les Éthiopiens de Gondar*, quoted here in *Miroir de l'Afrique*, Paris, Gallimard, 1996. First published in the collection 'L'Homme, Cahiers d'ethnologie, de géographie et de linguistique', Paris, Plon, 1958, nouvelle collection, No. 1.

9 Ibid., p. 1035.

10 Ibid., p. 963, and note 15.

11 Ibid., p. 958.

12 Ibid., p. 1023.

13 I pointed out in *Le Dieu objet* (Paris, Flammarion, 1988, p. 23), that one property of voodoo is to 'go to the head' of those who serve it. Besides the observation quoted, Maupoil gives a number of indications of this. Cf. Bernard Maupoil, *La Géomancie a l' ancienne côte des Esclaves*, Paris, Institut d' ethnologie, 1943, reprinted 1992, p. 59–60.

14 I am indebted for these observations and the comments that follow to Bertrand Feron's notes in his translation for Gallimard (*L'Inquiétante Étrangeté et autres Éssais*), in the 'Folio essais' collection, 1985) of the essays earlier collected and translated by Marie Bonaparte and Madame E. Marty under the title *Essais de psychanalyse appliquée* (Paris, Gallimard, 1933).

15 Sigmund Freud, 'Creative Writers and Day-Dreaming', in *Art and Literature*, Penguin Freud Library, vol. 14, trans. James Strachey, Harmondsworth, 1985, reprinted 1990, pp. 131–2.

16 Ibid., p. 132.

17 Ibid., p. 133.

18 Ibid., p. 136.

19 Ibid., p. 138.

20 Ibid., pp. 140–1.

21 Ibid., p. 138.

22 Ibid.

23 Ibid., p. 140.

24 Sigmund Freud, 'Delusions and Dreams in Jensen's *Gradiva*', in *Art and Literature*, p. 115.

25 J.-B. Pontalis, Preface, in Sigmund Freud, *Le Délire et les rêves dans la Gradiva de W. Jensen*, French translation, Paris, Gallimard, 1986, p. 21.

ANTECEDENTS: THE COLONISED IMAGE AND THE COLONISED DREAM

1 Serge Gruzinski, *La Guerre des images*, Paris, Fayard, 1990.

2 Jacques Le Goff, *L'Imaginaire médiéval*, Paris, Gallimard, 1985.

3 Jean-Claude Schmitt, *Les Revenants*, Paris, Gallimard, 1994.

4 Carlo Ginzburg, *Storia notturna: una decifrazione del sabba*, Turin, Einaudi, 1989.

5 Serge Gruzinski, in J.-M. Sallmann, *Visions indiennes, visions baroques: les métissages de l'inconscient*, Paris, PUF, 1992.

6 Ibid., p. 129.

7 Jean-Claude Schmitt, *Les Revenants*, p. 59.

8 Ibid., p. 60. This need to 'sort out' good from bad is also expressed by the head of the Department of Selection in the palace of dreams which Ismael Kadare took as an archetype of the thought police in his novel *The Palace of Dreams*, published in Albania in 1981: 'Firstly dreams of a private nature, with no relation to the State. Then the dreams which are provoked by hunger or satiety, cold or heat or illnesses, etc., in a word all those connected with the flesh. Lastly, simulated dreams, in other words the ones which weren't really seen, only imagined by some people in the hope of getting on in life, or concocted by mythomanes or provocateurs. But that's easier said than done! Flushing them out is no simple matter. A dream can appear to be of a private nature, or prompted by trivial purposes, while it is in fact directly connected to reasons of State ...' (translated from the French edition, Paris, Fayard, 1990).

9 Jean-Claude Schmitt, *Les Revenants*, p. 60.

10 Ibid., p. 51.

11 Ibid., p. 59.

12 We find references to the spectating self in Sartre and relating to composite individuals in Freud. Sartre: 'The presence of the *self* in dreams is frequent and almost necessary in the case of "deep" dreams, but one can cite numerous dreams immediately on falling asleep where the sleeper's self plays no part. Here is one, for example, which was told to me by Mademoiselle B...: the first thing that appeared was a plate from a book showing a slave at his

mistress's feet, then this slave went off in search of pus to cure himself of the leprosy which his mistress had given him; this had to be the pus of a woman who loved him. Throughout the dream the sleeper had the sensation of *reading* the narrative of the slave's adventures. At no point did she play any part in what was happening. It is moreover frequent that dreams – for instance, in my own case – present themselves at first as a story that I am reading or being told. And then, all of a sudden, I identify myself with one of the characters in the story, which becomes *my story* ...' (*L'Imaginaire*, Paris, Gallimard, 'Folio essais' collection, 1986, p. 52; first published, Gallimard, 1940).

Freud (on the work of *condensation*): 'On the one hand, the dream-figure may bear the name of one of the persons related to it – in which case we simply know directly, in a manner analogous to our waking knowledge, that this or that person is intended – while its visual features may belong to the other person. Or, on the other hand, the dream-image itself may be composed of visual features belonging in reality partly to the one person and partly to the other. Or again, the second person's share in the dream-image may lie, not in its visual features, but in the gestures that we attribute to it, the words that we make it speak, or the situation in which we place it' (*Interpretation of Dreams*, Chapter 6, London, Hogarth, 1955).

13 Jean-Claude Schmitt, *Les Revenants*, p. 64.
14 Carlo Ginzburg, *Storia notturna*, p. 251.
15 Ibid., pp. 288–9.
16 Serge Gruzinski, *La Guerre des images*, p. 241.
17 Ibid., p. 248.
18 Ibid., p. 154.
19 Ibid., p. 318.
20 Ibid.
21 Ibid., p. 325.

22 See Jean-Michel Sallmann (ed.) *Visions indiennes, visions baroques: les métissages de l'inconscient*, introduction.

23 Jean-François Lyotard, *La Condition postmoderne*, Paris, Éditions de Minuit, 1979 (*The Postmodern Condition: A Report on Knowledge*, trans. G. Bennington and B. Massumi, Manchester, Manchester University Press, 1984). Vincent Descombes, *Philosophie par gros temps*, Paris, Éditions de Minuit, 1989.

24 Marc Augé, *Pour une anthropologie des mondes contemporains*, Paris, Aubier, 1994.

25 Georges Balandier, *Sociologie actuelle de l' Afrique noire*, Paris, PUF, 1955.

26 Serge Gruzinski, *La Guerre des images*, p. 329.

27 Ibid., p. 331.

THE THEATRE OF OPERATIONS

1 Francisco Ferrandiz, 'Dimensions of Nationalism in a Venezuelan Possession Cult', *Kroeber Anthropological Society (KAS) Papers* 75–6, 1992, pp. 28–47; Daisy Barreto, 'Plasticité et résistance: le mythe et le culte de María Lionza au Venezuela', *Gradhiva* 15, 1994.

2 References here are to the third edition of *Le Signifiant imaginaire*, Paris, Bourgois, 1993. The two earlier editions date from 1977 and 1984.

3 'L'Illusion comique ou le théâtre du point de vue de l'imaginaire', in *Clefs pour l' imaginaire ou l'Autre Scène*, Paris, Éditions du Seuil, 1969.

4 Christian Metz, *Le Signifiant imaginaire,* p. 93.

5 Ibid., p. 94.

6 European actors sometimes do feature in American films or even build a career in the United States. But these

occurrences of short-lived or permanent assimilation do not affect the object of our analysis here.

7 Christian Metz, *Le Signifiant imaginaire,* p. 100.

8 Ibid., p. 120.

9 Ibid., p. 119.

10 Ibid., p. 126.

11 Ibid.

12 Ibid.

13 Ibid., p. 157.

14 Ibid., p. 144.

15 Ibid., p. 145.

16 Ibid., p. 137.

17 Ibid., p. 167.

18 Latest edition, 1994, Coop. Breizh, Rennes, Jeanne Laffitte.

19 To avoid the ambiguity of the term 'fictive' which has besides the meaning of 'deceptive', I propose the adjective 'fictional' to qualify any practice of 'fictionalisation'.

20 Jean-Pierre Vernant, *Entre mythe et politique,* Paris, Éditions du Seuil, 1996, pp. 237–52.

21 Pierre Bourdieu, Luc Boltanski, Robert Castel and Jean-Claude Chamboredon, *Un art moyen: essai sur les usages sociaux de la photographie,* Paris, Éditions de Minuit, 1965.

22 I have in mind most particularly an article by Vicente Verdu which appeared in a Caracas newspaper, *El Nacional,* on 19 December 1995.

23 The South American press keeps a close eye on the most spectacular displays of North American technology, perhaps because the majority of South American countries typify a situation in which hyper-modern technology co-exists with social underdevelopment – with the ideal of modernity linked to the ideal of independence remaining no more than an ideal. Some of the information which I have used in this paragraph derives from the Caracas newspaper *El Nacional.*

THE AGENDA

1 Jean-Paul Sartre, *L'Imaginaire*, Paris, Gallimard, 1940, quoted in the 'Folio essais' collection, 1986, p. 339.

Index